WELSH HISTORY AND I

D1627859

Edward I and Wales

Edward I and Wales

Edited by

Trevor Herbert
Gareth Elwyn Jones

Cardiff
University of Wales Press
1988

University of Wales Press, 6 Gwennyth Street, Cathays, Cardiff CF2 4YD

British Library Cataloguing in Publication Data

Edward I and Wales.
  Wales. History
  I. Herbert, Trevor II. Jones, Gareth Elwyn
  942.9

ISBN 0-7083-1012-5

Cover Design : Cloud Nine Design.
The publishers wish to acknowledge the advice and assistance given by the Design Department of the Welsh Books Council which is supported by the Welsh Arts Council.

Typeset by Megaron, Cardiff.

Printed in Wales by Graham Harcourt (Printers) Ltd, Swansea

Welsh History and its Sources

Welsh History and its Sources is a project conducted at the Open University in Wales from 1985 to 1988 and funded by a Welsh Office Research Development grant. The project gratefully acknowledges the financial support made available by the Secretary of State for Wales.

Project Director:	Dr Trevor Herbert
Senior Visiting Fellow:	Dr Gareth Elwyn Jones
Steering Committee:	Mr O.E. Jones, H.M.I. (Chairman)
	Professor R.R. Davies, History Department, University College of Wales, Aberystwyth
	Mr N. Evans, Coleg Harlech
	Mr D. Maddox, Adviser, Mid Glamorgan LEA
	Mr A. Evans, Head of History Department, Y Pant Comprehensive School, Pontyclun
Secretary to the Project at the Open University in Wales:	Mrs Julia Williams

Contents

Illustrations

Maps and Diagrams

The Contributors

Trevor Herbert is Sub-Dean of Arts and Senior Lecturer in Music at the Open University, and Staff Tutor in Arts at the Open University in Wales.

Gareth Elwyn Jones is Reader in History Education at University College of Swansea and an Open University tutor-counsellor for the arts foundation course.

J. Beverley Smith is Sir John Williams Professor of Welsh History at the University College of Wales, Aberystwyth.

Ifor Rowlands is Lecturer in History at the University College of Swansea.

Llinos Beverley Smith is Lecturer in Welsh History at the University College of Wales, Aberystwyth.

Glanmor Williams is Emeritus Professor of History, University College of Swansea.

A.D. Carr is Senior Lecturer and Head of the Department of Welsh History at the University College of North Wales, Bangor.

Robert Morris is Education Officer for CADW, Welsh Historic Monuments.

R.R. DAVIES is Professor of History at the University College of Wales, Aberystwyth and a member of the Welsh History and its Sources project Steering Committee.

The Preface, **Debating the Evidence** and Glossary sections of this book have been written by Robert Morris.

Preface

This series gives an insight into Welsh history by examining its sources and the ways in which some leading historians use those sources. It is not formally a history of Wales. This volume, for instance, is not a chronological history of medieval Wales, neither is it a comprehensive history in the sense that its themes embrace all of the major issues and events that were important in that period. Readers of this book will, we hope, learn a great deal about Wales in the thirteenth century but they will learn as much about the way in which professional historians interpret the raw materials of history.

The choice of topics for the essays and the collections of documents was determined as much by the nature of the sources relevant to those topics as by the subject matter of the events or issues upon which they are based. Nevertheless, the various sections give a coherent, if not comprehensive, profile of the period.

The thirteenth century was a 'climacteric' in the history of Wales. The Edwardian conquest of 1282–4 cut across a pattern of internal development that seemed to be well established as late as the early 1270s. The work of Llywelyn ab Iorwerth up to 1240 appeared to augur well for the creation of a minor *feudal* state in Wales based upon Gwynedd. Llywelyn created a network of dependency within Wales which involved most of the native princes and lords. Yet his work depended above all on the Crown of England being unable or unwilling to exert its full strength as a military power and *feudal* overlord in Wales. Since the time of Hywel Dda in the tenth century, Welsh rulers had sworn *fealty* to the kings of England, and although effective royal control seldom reached into the fastnesses of Gwynedd, the claim to full *feudal* overlordship always gave the kings of England a powerful leverage in Welsh politics.

The notorious fractiousness of the Welsh lords in their relations with each other bedevilled any attempt by one of their own number to win overall dominance within Wales. Gwynedd saw itself historically as a kingdom rather than a lordship — the successor state to Rhodri Mawr's eighth-century hegemony. Its claim to pre-eminence, however, was not readily accepted by other Welsh rulers. Most of the Welsh lords claimed descent from one or other of the Dark-Age royal houses of Wales. Rulers of Deheubarth, descended from Rhys ap Tewdwr and Hywel Dda, regarded their state as fully equal to that of the princes of Gwynedd. The rulers of Gwynedd could never be more than a 'keystone in an arch of kings'. Full political unity in Wales may have been closer than ever before, but the prospect was still pretty remote. The term 'Wales' was hardly valid even as a geographical expression — since the country's geography was one of the main obstacles to unity.

It was military prowess, shrewd leadership and skilful administration, coupled with its more secure geographical position in relation to England, that gave the rulers of Gwynedd an edge over other Welsh lordships by the thirteenth century. Powys, heir in name to a large, lost kingdom of the Dark Ages, had become essentially a Marcher lordship by the thirteenth century. Its rulers, like their Anglo-Norman neighbours, guarded their old but vulnerable prerogatives with the utmost jealousy. A distant overlord — the king — whose *feudal* pre-eminence was unquestionable, was usually preferable to an interventionist prince whose lightning forays across the Berwyns were all too real a threat.

Llywelyn ap Gruffudd was a skilled leader who inherited the traditional claims of Gwynedd and who possessed the skill and determination to advance those claims to the highest state of fruition they were ever to achieve. From the nadir of 1247, when Gwynedd was effectively partitioned, to the Treaty of Montgomery in 1267, Llywelyn won for himself a unique position as the king's chief *vassal*, the acknowledged Prince of Wales, owing *fealty* to the king for his principality. Yet Llywelyn is not remembered for this signal triumph; rather he is recalled as 'Llywelyn the Last' — casualty of the final cataclysm — whose impaled head was exhibited in London. He has been eulogized as the innocent victim of a Machiavellian ruler and as the martyr of an embryonic Welsh nationhood. But he has also been cast as a flawed Oresteian figure whose political judgement was warped by overwhelming ambition, until he finally incurred the righteous wrath and retribution of Edward I. The two essays by J. Beverley Smith and

Ifor Rowlands look behind these deceptively plausible images. They show the scope for conflict that was inherent in the contrary policies followed by both Llywelyn and Edward I from the early 1270s on, emphasizing the volatility introduced into a difficult relationship by the Marcher barons and disaffected Welsh lords. Especial importance must be accorded to the 'rogue factor' of Dafydd ap Gruffudd. Was he the traitor who gave Edward I one of his strongest trump cards against Llywelyn and who personally provoked the final tragedy of 1282? Or was he the frustrated cat's-paw of Llywelyn's dynastic aggrandizement, caught between the devil and the deep blue sea and desperately seeking help wherever it was offered?

Llinos Beverley Smith analyses the nature of the regime that the conquest introduced into Wales, the elements of continuity with Welsh custom and law, the innovations that were made and the thinking that motivated them. The administrative structure on which Edwardian governance rested was essentially a robust skeleton of law fleshed out by the personal discretion and judgement of royal officials on the spot and constrained by local conditions and attitudes. This is a common characteristic of many colonial regimes. Edward's policy towards the Welsh was, at times, repressive and, at others, conciliatory. The Madog ap Llywelyn rebellion of 1295 placed especial strain upon the new order — it put the government under pressure to be more draconian and it also provoked fears among the Welsh of 'racial backlash' from their new masters.

Edward I himself generally presents a statesmanlike image of fairness, although the actions of his officials, several days' ride from court, often show a different picture. Which was the immediate reality which the Welsh people saw? A.D. Carr shows how Welsh communities reacted to the new conditions in which they found themselves. He emphasizes how the Edwardian regime — and any other form of medieval rule — required more than docile acquiescence on the part of its subjects at grass-roots level. Indeed, medieval society was so patently lacking in docility that only a high level of involvement by those with land and the rights and obligations that derived from land could stave off chaos. It was not a time to be a 'quiet-lifer'. Records of complaints, petitions and legal actions show the reality of life in colonial Wales as the ordinances and statutes cannot. These show people dealing with the day-to-day problems the change of rulers may have created for them — as well as problems they would have faced anyway. Recent research has shown the surprisingly dogged continuity of land tenure in various parts of Wales up to the eighteenth century. This tenacity underlines the factor which was fundamental to every individual in a society in flux — the will to survive. Native Welsh society did survive — it was hardy enough and angry enough to erupt into a widespread revolt over a century after the conquest.

Glanmor Williams demonstrates the all-pervading influence of the Church on medieval life, and the far-reaching secular influence the Church wielded. As the guardian of Christian truth the Church was accorded a respect that appears strangely at odds with such a violent society. Yet today's world shows that violence and extremes of religious devotion are never far apart. There was nothing ecumenical about religious zeal in the Middle Ages, and tolerance was not regarded as a virtue. It was a paradox, even in medieval terms, that the highest form of Christian service open to a layman was to go to war — to fight in the Crusade. But it was a paradox that the Church understood very well — man's basic aggression was being sublimated into an overtly religious mission. Edward I was himself a Crusader and accepted the paradox of the Christian warrior at face value.

This acceptance made it all the easier for kings and their dependent clergy to see their political enemies as enemies of the Church and of true religion. The vitriolic condemnation of Llywelyn which many clerical chroniclers and clerical writers indulged in are more comprehensible in this light. The tightrope the Bishops of Bangor and St Asaph had to walk in preserving the rights of their sees in the face of an increasingly demanding Gwynedd polity, in reserving their obedience to Canterbury, now hand-in-glove with the English Crown, while serving dioceses that were ruled by a strong Welsh prince at odds with that same Crown, come vividly to life in these documents. The spiritual quality of religious life may have declined from the reforming peaks of Cluniac and Cistercian monastic reform movements of the tenth to the twelfth centuries, but religious zeal was as sincere as ever, as *Gerald of Wales* testifies in his own acerbic style.

Ifor Rowlands's essay examines the relative strengths and weaknesses of the opposing forces in the wars of 1277 and 1282–3. He analyses the strategy of Edward I and how Llywelyn appears to have tried to strengthen his military position without provoking the very conflict he sought to avoid. In any study of military history, especially one of such a remote date, the surviving evidence is inevitably slanted towards the victor. Hermann Goering commented at Nuremberg in 1946 that 'the victors are always the judges, and it is the vanquished who are punished'. A Nazi leader is a very dubious interpreter of either judicial or historical fairness, but the above comment should not lightly be dismissed. The impressive array of evidence that has survived of Edward I's military organization is in itself proof of the emphasis he placed on sound logistics as opposed to the masterly coup on the field of battle. The importance of naval strength is also shown very clearly, and in any arms race the relative rate of resources-drainage on participating countries is a vital factor. Llywelyn's Gwynedd was clearly dependent on its traditional resources — natural defensibility, enhanced by a programme of castle-building which the *Marcher lords* and the Crown did their utmost to thwart.

The rival strategies of the war of 1282 are explored, taking into account the notorious difficulty of discerning Llywelyn's overall military objectives through the all-obscuring cataract of *Cilmeri*. The colossal feats of military engineering which consolidated Edward's conquest in north Wales bring a new dimension to the deployment of historical evidence. The castles themselves remain the most concrete and tangible testaments imaginable to the scale of Edward's operations and the importance he attached to the conquest of Wales. The study of the easily accessible archaeological evidence which castles open to the public can offer is one that should be embraced as part of any treatment of this period.

At one level *Edward I and Wales* is simply a book about the history of Wales at a time when a number of fundamental changes were taking place, and about the ways in which historians interpret that period. However, the series of which this volume is a part has been designed to serve a number of functions for anyone who is formally or informally engaged in a study of Welsh history. Those studying with a tutor, for instance extra-mural, university or sixth-form students, will find that it is a resource which will form a basis for, or enhance, a broader study of Welsh history. Those who are studying in a more remote location, far from formal classes in Welsh history, will find that the contents of the book are so ordered as to guide them through a course of study similar, but not analogous, to the methods which have proved successful in continuing education programmes of the Open University. The main feature of this method is that it attempts to combine a programmatic approach with something more flexible and open-ended.

Central to this book are Sections A to E which contain three different but closely related and interlinked types of material. Each of the five essays is written on a clearly defined topic. Each essay is immediately followed by a collection of source material which is the basis of the evidence for the essay. Within each essay, reference is made to a particular source document by the inclusion of a reference number in the essay text; this reference number is also placed in the left-hand margin of the essay.

The sources section is followed by a 'discussion' of the topic. The primary purpose here is to highlight the special features, weaknesses and strengths of each collection of sources and to question the way in which the author of the essay has used them. It is worth pointing out that we have not attempted here simply to act as *agents provocateurs*, setting up a series of artificial controversies which can be comfortably demolished. The purpose is to raise the sorts of questions which the essayists themselves probably addressed before they employed these sources. In doing this we hope to expose the types of issues that the historian has to deal with. The discussion sections pose a number of questions about the sources. They do not provide model answers and neatly tie up all of the loose ends concerning each source. The discipline of history does not allow that approach. If it did, there would be no need for a book of this type. The 'discussions' simply put forward a number of ideas which will cause readers to consider and reconsider the issues which have been raised. The purpose is to breed the kind of healthy scepticism about historical sources which underlies the method of approach of the professional historian.

Other parts of the book support these central sections. The Introduction poses basic problems about the difficulties of coping with historical sources, points which are consolidated in the Discussion sections. The intention of the opening essay, 'Edward I and Wales', is to outline the principal changes which took place in Wales during this period and to hint at the issues that motivated those changes.

At the end of the book is a glossary which explains briefly a number of the more technical terms and concepts arising out of the essays/sources collection. Although a glossary is properly a list of explanations of words and terms, we have additionally included brief details of persons who are prominent in the essay and source material. Any word *italicized* (thus) in the text will be explained in the glossary.

Readers will, of course, decide how best to profit from the different constituent elements in the book. The first two chapters should certainly be read first, as these provide a context for the rest of the book. Some may then decide to read the five essays without reference to the source collections or discussion sections. This will form a broader framework for a re-examination of the essays with their sources and discussion sections.

The open-ended nature of the book serves to highlight the extent to which it has been our intention to do no more than *contribute* to an understanding of Welsh history. Different editors would have chosen different topics. The essays here should be seen within the framework of a much wider range of writings which, over the past few decades, has become available. The greatest success which a book like this can meet with is that it imparts to its readers an insatiable desire to know more about Welsh history and to do so from a standpoint which is constantly and intelligently questioning the ways in which historians provide that knowledge.

Acknowledgements

The development of the Welsh History and its Sources project was made possible by the support of the Secretary of State for Wales and I am happy to have made formal acknowledgement to the Secretary of State and individuals connected with the project elsewhere in this book.

Funding from the Open University made possible the development of the initial ideas that were eventually nurtured by a Welsh Office grant. The assistance of various individuals and departments of the Open University has been frequently and freely given. In particular, I am grateful to Wynne Brindle, Richard McKracken and Barry Hollis. Also my colleagues at the Open University in Wales, where the project was based, have been constantly helpful. Julia Williams, secretary to the Arts Faculty of the Open University in Wales, acted as secretary to the project. As well as word-processing the texts for the series she was immensely efficient in the administration of the project. Sandra Bewick, also of the Open University in Wales, word-processed a substantial amount of this volume with painstaking accuracy.

The University College of Swansea were kind enough to allow the part secondment of Dr Gareth Elwyn Jones to work on the project. Without him the project would not have progressed beyond being an idea as I have relied entirely on his widely respected expertise for overseeing the academic content of the series.

I also wish to express my gratitude to Professor R.R. Davies of the University College of Wales, Aberystwyth, whose careful reading of the drafts led to major changes in the pedagogical sections of this book.

Diverse contributions have enhanced the effectiveness of the material. The maps and diagrams were redesigned from various sources by Professor David Herbert and drawn by Guy Lewis, both of the Department of Geography, University College of Swansea.

Photographic research and administration were done by Rhodri Morgan. Ceinwen Jones of the University of Wales Press copy-edited this volume and made many useful suggestions for improvement.

My major debt of gratitude is to the contributors, each of whom was asked to write to a prescribed topic, format, word length and submission date. Each fulfilled the brief with absolute accuracy, punctuality and co-operation. The format was prescribed by me. Any shortcomings that remain can be put down to that prescription and to the consequences that emanated from it.

TREVOR HERBERT
Cardiff
March 1988

Introduction

The essays contained in this book have been written not only by specialist historians, but also by specialists in the particular topic on which they have written. They are authorities on their subject and they make pertinent, informed and professional observations. Each essay is an important contribution to the historiography of Wales.

As specialists they know the sources for their topics intimately. They have included extracts from a cross-section of these sources to indicate on what evidence they base the generalizations and conclusions in their essays. We hope that the essays will interest you and that the documents will bring you into contact with the kind of primary sources which you may not have encountered before. Historians face a variety of problems when they consult source material and face even more difficulties when they have to synthesize the material collected into a coherent narrative and analysis of the events they are describing. In doing so, even the best historians make mistakes. Sometimes these are trivial (or not so trivial!) errors of fact. You may even spot factual discrepancies between information given in the various essays and the documents in this book.

At the end of each essay/sources section there is a short Debating the Evidence section. By the time you reach it you will have read the essay and the sources on which the essay is based.

The Debating the Evidence section is concerned with problems of interpretation. It is an attempt to conduct a debate with the author about the way in which the essay relates to the sources. This is partly achieved by asking pertinent questions about the nature of the sources. The intention is that you are stimulated to think about the validity of the exercise of writing history and the methodology of the study of history which is essentially what distinguishes it from other disciplines. The dialogue is a complex one and the questions posed do not, generally, have any 'right' answers. But they do have some answers which make more sense than others. We feel that the historians who have written the essays have provided answers which are reasonable. But historians are not infallible, however eminent they may be. Their conclusions are open to debate and discussion, as, for that matter, is their whole procedure of working. As you work through the discussion and questions you will notice that there is specific cross-referencing to the relevant section of the essay (or essays) and to sources. It is important that you use these cross-references since the success of the exercise depends vitally on taking into account the relationship between the primary source material and what the historian makes of it.

At the heart of the historian's task is the search for and subsequent use of evidence, much of it of the sort you will encounter here. The crucial distinction in the nature of this evidence is that between primary and secondary sources. There is no completely watertight definition of what constitutes a primary source but a reasonable working definition would be that primary sources consist of material which came into existence during the particular period which the historian is researching, while secondary sources came into existence after that period. Another important point is that the extent to which a source can be regarded as primary or secondary relies as much on the topic of research as it does on the date of that source.

The vast majority of the documents which the authors use in the ensuing chapters are in print, as can be seen from the attributions. There are exceptions. For example, Dr Llinos Smith refers to the original of a document in the British Library (C.12) which she has consulted and transcribed. The British Library is an important repository of original documents relating to thirteenth-century Wales, as are the National Library of Wales and the Public Record Office. Obviously, printed versions are more accessible and are the product of scholars having, perhaps, transcribed, edited, translated and calendared the relevant documents. The originals remain sovereign, but expert historians know well in which editors they can place their trust and the material reproduced in this volume is extremely reliable. However, it is worth remembering that it is some way removed from the original material written down in, say, 1282. It has been transcribed and typeset on at least two occasions before appearing on the page you read and we all know how easily inaccuracies can creep in to these processes. All students of history need to remind themselves of the exact status of printed primary sources, though primary sources they remain. The secondary sources referred to in this book are among those which appear in the section on Further Reading.

The interpretation of historical sources is extremely complex. It was once believed by highly reputable historians that if they mastered all the sources they could write 'true' history. There is at least one eminent historian who argues this now. You might like to consider on which side of the debate you stand at the moment.

Most historians would argue that this is impossible. Because we are removed from the time and place of the event, we are influenced by prejudices of nationality, religion or politics. However, there is some compensation for this because we know, usually, what the results were of actions which occurred during the period of a given topic and this benefit of hindsight is enormously useful in trying to analyse the interplay of various factors in a situation and their influence on subsequent events. As you read the essays and documents in this collection, consider the degree of objectivity and subjectivity displayed by the authors. To do this you will need to consider what you would like to know about the authors before coming to a decision and how far the authors are entitled to their own interpretations. Of course, you, too, may come to the material with your own prejudices.

There is a similar pattern of presentation for each essay and its related documents. There are specific questions involving comprehension, evaluation, interpretation and synthesis, with synthesis, arguably, the highest level of the skills. However, there can be no rigid demarcation of historical skills such as interpretation and synthesis and some questions will overlap the various categories. Neither is there a standard form of 'answer', as the discussions demonstrate. What the questions do provide is guidance for a structured pattern of study which will enhance your understanding of the essays and documents.

Above all, there is dialogue and discussion about the way in which each historian has handled the complexities of writing about and interpreting the past. That such interpretation is as skilled, informed and mature as is conceivably possible is essential to our well-being as a society. In that these books are about the history of Wales they contribute fundamentally to that end. That vitality depends on debate — analytical, informed, structured debate. It is the purpose of this book to stimulate your involvement in that debate in a more structured way than has been attempted before in the study of the history of Wales.

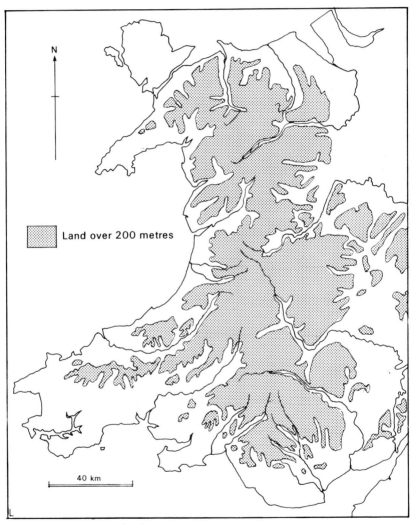

Principal physical features of Wales.

Timechart

Wales		Other Significant Events
Civil War in Gwynedd: Llywelyn ab Iorwerth becomes dominant in north-east Wales.	1194	
Death of the Lord Rhys in Deheubarth.	1197	
	1199	Death of Richard I: succession of King John.
Llywelyn ab Iorwerth wins control of west Gwynedd.	1201	
Llywelyn marries King John's daughter Joan (Siwan).	1205	
	1206	Pope nominates Stephen Langton to Canterbury.
	1208	England under Papal Interdict.
King John invades Gwynedd.	1211	
	1213	King John's accord with Papacy.
	1215	Magna Carta.
	1216	Death of King John. Minority of Henry III.

Treaty of Worcester: recognition of Llwyelyn's primacy in Wales as vassal of king.	**1218**	
	1219	Death of William Marshal: pre-eminence of Hubert de Burgh as royal guardian.
Llywelyn adopts style 'Prince of Aberffraw and Lord of Eryri'. First imprisonment of elder son Gruffudd.	**1228**	
	1232	Fall of Hubert de Burgh.
Treaty of Middle between Henry III and Llywelyn.	**1234**	
Welsh lords and princes pay homage to Dafydd ap Llywelyn as Llywelyn's heir at Strata Florida.	**1238**	
Death of Llywelyn: Dafydd's succession challenged by Gruffudd ap Llywelyn: Gruffudd imprisoned by Dafydd.	**1240**	Simon de Montfort, king's brother-in-law, exiled in disgrace.
Defeat of Dafydd by Henry III: Treaty of Gwern Eigron: shiring of Cardigan and Carmarthen. Gruffudd transferred to king's custody.	**1241**	
Gruffudd killed in escape bid from Tower of London.	**1244**	Lords in Parliament protest against Henry III's personal government.
Rising by Dafydd. Henry III's campaign in north Wales fails at Degannwy.	**1245**	

Death of Dafydd: Gwynedd divided between Gruffudd's elder sons, Owain and Llywelyn.	**1246**	
Treaty of Woodstock: Gwynedd deprived of homage of other Welsh lords, north-east Wales lost to Crown and partitioning of Gwynedd recognized.	**1247**	
Llywelyn ap Gruffudd defeats Owain and allies at Bryn Derwin.	**1255**	Parliament demands right to appoint royal ministers.
Llywelyn and his brother Dafydd regain north-east Wales.	**1256**	
Llywelyn makes a pact with the Scots; he adopts style 'Prince of Wales'.	**1258**	Simon de Montfort leads baronial opposition to Henry III and forces him to concede Provisions of Oxford.
Llywelyn controls mid-Wales; Dafydd ap Gruffudd joins king.	**1263**	
	1264	De Montfort wins Battle of Lewes: the King and Lord Edward captured.
Treaty of Pipton between Llywelyn and Simon de Montfort.	**1265**	Escape of Lord Edward; defeat and death of Simon at Evesham.
Treaty of Montgomery: recognition of Llywelyn as Prince of Wales.	**1267**	
Llywelyn secures homage of Maredudd ap Rhys.	**1270**	

	1272	Death of Henry III: Edward I succeeds to throne while away on crusade.
Llywelyn fails to swear fealty to Edward at Montgomery Ford; Edward's regents instruct Llywelyn to stop building Dolforwyn Castle.	**1273**	Edward I in Gascony.
Dafydd and Gruffudd ap Gwenwynwyn plot to assassinate Llywelyn.	**1274**	Edward I's return to England and coronation: the King summons Llywelyn to do homage.
Gruffudd ap Gwenwynwyn raids Wales from Shrewsbury.	**1275**	Eleanor de Montfort married to Llywelyn by proxy, captured *en route* to Wales and detained in England. Archbishop Kilwardby confirms rights of St Asaph diocese in dispute between Bishop Anian and Llywelyn.
Llywelyn fails for third time to come to do homage to the King.	**1276**	Archbishop Kilwardby attempts a mediation between Edward and Llywelyn; Edward declares war on Llywelyn as 'a rebel and disturber of his peace'.
Edward I invades Wales: defeat and submission of Llywelyn. Treaty of Aberconwy: Llywelyn swears fealty and does homage to King. Royal castles established at Flint, Rhuddlan and Aberystwyth.	**1277**	

Emergence of Arwystli dispute with Gruffudd ap Gwenwynwyn.	1278	Llywelyn married to Eleanor de Montfort at Worcester in King's presence; Archbishop Pecham supports Bishop Anian of Bangor in dispute with Llywelyn.
Royal commissions of inquiry into Arwystli dispute; Robert Tibetot Justiciar of West Wales.	1280–1	
Dafydd ap Gruffudd's Palm Sunday revolt; Anglesey captured by Edward; failure of de Tany's amphibious landing; Llywelyn strikes at mid-Wales; death of Llywelyn at Cilmeri.	1282	Edward raises feudal host to invade Wales; Archbishop Pecham's mediation attempt.
Conquest of Gwynedd; new royal castles at Conwy, Caernarfon and Harlech; Cricieth rebuilt; capture and execution of Dafydd ap Gruffudd.	1283	
Statute of Rhuddlan: Welsh shires and sheriffs appointed; Otto de Granson appointed Justice of North Wales; Archbishop Pecham's visitation to Welsh dioceses.	1284	Birth of Prince Edward of Caernarfon.
	1286	Death of King Alexander III of Scotland.
Revolt of Rhys ap Maredudd.	1287	
	1290	Expulsion of Jews from England; death of Queen Margaret of Scotland.

	1291–3	Development of conflict between England and Scotland.
Revolt of Madog ap Llywelyn; work begins on Beaumaris Castle.	**1294–5**	'Model Parliament' at Westminster.
Repair and rebuilding of Welsh castles under way.	**1296**	Edward I defeats Scots at Dunbar.
	1298	Defeat of Wallace.
John de Havering Justice of Principality of Wales.	**1300**	
Edward of Caernarfon invested as Prince of Wales.	**1301**	
	1303	Renewed war in Scotland.
Welsh petitions to Prince Edward at Kennington.	**1305**	Capture and execution of Wallace.
	1306	Robert Bruce rebels in Scotland.
	1307	Death of Edward I at Carlisle.
	1308–13	Edward II's court torn by the Piers Gaveston issue.
Payn de Turberville granted lordship of Glamorgan.	**1314**	Robert Bruce defeats English armies at Bannockburn.
Revolt of Llywelyn Bren against Turberville in Glamorgan.	**1316**	
Llywelyn Bren put to death by Hugh Despenser.	**1317**	
Welsh forces support King in civil war against Mortimer faction; Welsh led by Sir Gruffudd Llwyd and Rhys ap Gruffudd.	**1322**	24 Welsh members attend Parliament at York.

Edward II at Cardiff, Caerphilly Castle, Margam Abbey and Neath Castle; King captured at Llantrisant; royal treasure seized at Caerphilly by Queen Isabella and Mortimer.	**1326**	Despensers (father and son) executed by Queen's forces.
Sir Gruffudd Llwyd refuses to answer writ to attend deposition Parliament; Rhys ap Gruffudd's scheme to liberate Edward II is thwarted.	**1327**	Parliament deposes Edward II; 48 Welsh members attend session. Edward II murdered at Berkeley Castle.
Release of Sir Gruffudd Llwyd and Sir Hywel ap Gruffudd, former supporters of Edward II.	**1330**	Edward III's coup against Queen Isabella and Mortimer; Mortimer executed.
Murder of Henry de Shaldeford in north Wales.	**1345**	
	1346	Battle of Crécy: 5,000 Welsh troops under the Black Prince take part in the victory; Rhys ap Gruffudd and Hywel ap Gruffudd (y Fwyall) knighted.

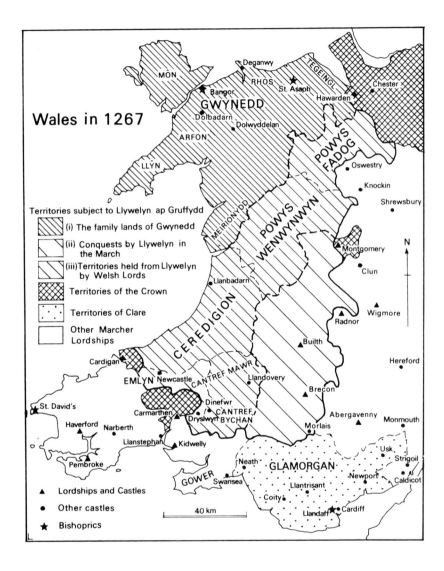

Wales in 1267

Territories subject to Llywelyn ap Gruffydd

- (i) The family lands of Gwynedd
- (ii) Conquests by Llywelyn in the March
- (iii) Territories held from Llywelyn by Welsh Lords

Territories of the Crown

Territories of Clare

Other Marcher Lordships

▲ Lordships and Castles
● Other castles
★ Bishoprics

40 km

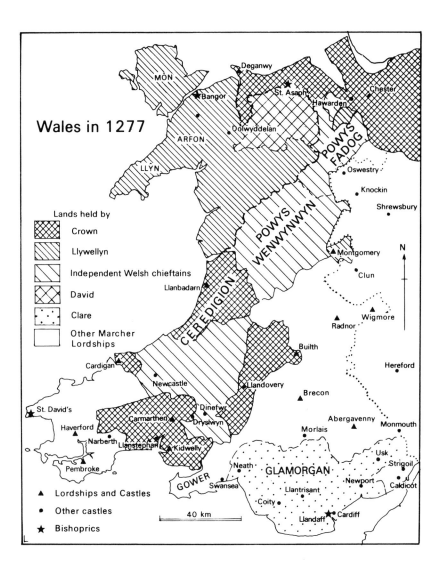

Wales in 1277

Lands held by

Crown

Llywellyn

Independent Welsh chieftains

David

Clare

Other Marcher Lordships

▲ Lordships and Castles

● Other castles

★ Bishoprics

40 km

N

MÔN
ARFON
LLYN
Deganwy
Bangor
St. Asaph
Chester
Hawarden
Dolwyddelan
POWYS FADOG
Oswestry
Knockin
Shrewsbury
POWYS WENWYNWYN
Montgomery
Clun
Llanbadarn
CEREDIGION
Wigmore
Radnor
Builth
Cardigan
Newcastle
Llandovery
Hereford
St. David's
Dinefwr
Brecon
Haverford
Carmarthen
Drysłwyn
Abergavenny
Monmouth
Narberth
Llanstephan
Kidwelly
Morlais
Usk
Strigoil
Pembroke
Neath
GLAMORGAN
Newport
Caldicot
GOWER
Swansea
Llantrisant
Coity
Llandaff
Cardiff

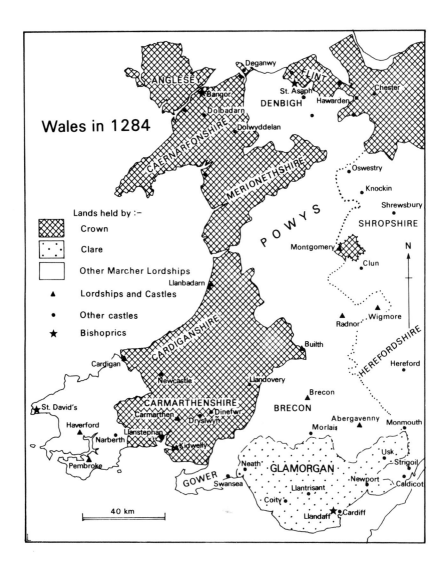

Wales in 1284

Lands held by :—

Crown

Clare

Other Marcher Lordships

▲ Lordships and Castles

● Other castles

★ Bishoprics

40 km

ANGLESEY
Deganwy
FLINT
St. Asaph
Chester
Bangor
Hawarden
Dolbadarn
DENBIGH
CAERNARFONSHIRE
Dolwyddelan
MERIONETHSHIRE
POWYS
Oswestry
Knockin
Shrewsbury
SHROPSHIRE
Montgomery
Clun
N
Llanbadarn
CARDIGANSHIRE
Radnor
Wigmore
Builth
HEREFORDSHIRE
Cardigan
Hereford
Newcastle
Llandovery
Brecon
St. David's
CARMARTHENSHIRE
BRECON
Carmarthen
Dinefwr
Abergavenny
Monmouth
Haverford
Dryslwyn
Morlais
Narberth
Llanstephan
Usk
Strigoil
Pembroke
Kidwelly
Neath
GLAMORGAN
Newport
Caldicot
GOWER
Swansea
Llantrisant
Coity
Llandaff
Cardiff

Edward I and Wales

R.R. DAVIES

Conquest and foreign domination are the themes of this volume. They are probably the most traumatic experiences that any country can undergo. Medieval Wales is no exception. The impact of the final Edwardian conquest of Wales 1277–83 was, it is true, greatly reduced by the fact that much of eastern and southern Wales had already been conquered in a piecemeal fashion over two centuries; the inhabitants of those districts had thereby had ample opportunity to come to terms with Anglo-Norman rule over many generations. Even in the rest of Wales the prospect of foreign conquest had loomed dangerously close on several occasions in the twelfth and thirteenth centuries. Nevertheless the shattering impact of the events of 1277–83 on north and west Wales and on what we may call the Welsh national psyche can hardly be denied. 'Is it the end of the world?' (*Oes derfyn byd?*), wondered one poet in a mood of suicidal despair; 'Ah God, that the sea would drown the land!' (*Och hyd atat-ti, Dduw, na ddaw mor dros dir!*) yearned another (Source B.16). The native Welsh chronicler was more prosaic, but the telegraphic brevity of his comment could not conceal his sense of utter cataclysm: 'And then all Wales was cast to the ground' (*Ac yna y bwriwyd holl Gymru i'r llawr*).

It is not difficult to understand this hysterical response. Within the space of five years the three great Welsh princely dynasties of Gwynedd, Deheubarth and northern Powys were either virtually extinguished or peremptorily dispossessed or, at best, their surviving members were reduced to the status of distressed gentlefolk. Such dispossession and demotion were not only a tragedy for the families concerned; they also severed those ties of service, loyalty, patronage and reward which were the very cement of medieval social relations. A new governmental dispensation, with its centres at Caernarfon, Carmarthen and Chester, was installed; new offices and units, notably the shire and its *sheriff*, created; new surveys of financial dues compiled; and at the higher echelons of governance a new, exclusively non-Welsh administrative cadre took over the running of the conquered lands. This edifice of foreign rule was crowned by a new legal dispensation grandly proclaimed in the Statute of Wales in March 1284. There was much that was enlightened, tolerant and non-discriminating in the Statute, notably its permissive attitude towards Welsh legal procedures and inheritance customs. Nevertheless its purpose was clear: to introduce the Welsh, partly by command and partly by persuasion, to the superior habits of English law. It was 'in defence of their laws', as an English chronicler put it, that the Welsh had risen in revolt in 1282; part of the price of defeat was that they now had 'the law of London', as it came to be called contemptuously, foisted upon them. It is little wonder that a distinguished English historian should have referred to the Statute of Wales as 'the first colonial constitution'.

Conquest also meant foreign occupation. Garrisons were posted and, above all, castles were built or rebuilt throughout Wales. The mighty walls of Harlech or Denbigh, of Conway or Chirk still proclaim today more eloquently than any document the determination of the conquerors who built them and the irreversibility of their achievement. Within a generation or so those castles became expensive white elephants but not before they had performed a vital military and, above all, psychological function. They not only, in the words of a contemporary, 'contained and thwarted the attacks of the Welsh', but also literally petrified them into subjection. Their physical and metaphorical domination of the Welsh countryside was the most visible and, thereby, the most effective reminder of the power and permanence of English conquest. In the words of a later Welsh poet they were 'the tower of the bold conqueror' (*tŵr dewr goncwerwr*) (Essay B).

The borough was the civilian arm of this military rule. Indeed, in the long run the boroughs founded by Edward I and his magnates in Wales proved to be more effective and more offensive emblems of conquest and privilege than the castles. Built in the shadows of those castles, defended by their own strong walls, peopled by immigrant English *burgesses* and endowed with the most extensive commercial monopolies over their hinterlands, they quickly became the epitome of privileged exclusiveness and the most bitterly resented bastions of English rule. At the time of the conquest itself, the king had been advised that herding the Welsh into towns would be the quickest way to civilize them; but the reverse happened. Formally, though much less so in practice, Welshmen were excluded from the newly founded towns and, thereby, from the rich commercial privileges enjoyed by the *burgesses*. So it was that Welshmen came to feel outsiders in their own country. Their sense of exclusion was compounded by the stories and mythology of a new dispossession. By the standards of medieval, let alone modern, conquest, Edward I's victory in Wales was not followed by a massive campaign of expropriation. Nevertheless every conquest leaves its scars and memories; that of Wales was no exception. The most flourishing borough of native Wales, Llan-faes in Anglesey, and one of the premier abbeys of Wales, Aberconwy, were both demolished to suit Edward's strategic convenience; in Denbigh, more than ten thousand acres of the most fertile lands of the Clwyd basin were bestowed on settlers from Lancashire and Yorkshire, while the original Welsh holders of the land were forcibly resettled in distant and often poor parts of the lordship, just as a royal official in Glamorgan was later encouraged to remove the Welsh from the lowlands so that they could be replaced by English immigrants. Incidents such as these may have been few in number; but they are easily magnified in the folk memory and are the very stuff from which national paranoia and resentment are manufactured.

Yet it might be argued that Wales for generations had lived on the edge of conquest and had become familiar with, and indeed hardened to, the experiences that came in the wake of conquest. Should not Welshmen therefore have adjusted fairly rapidly and smoothly to the final conquest when it came? There is, of course, a considerable element of truth in these comments; but they also overlook the dramatic changes which had taken place within Wales in the two or three generations before the Edwardian conquest. It is on this issue that historians of medieval Wales have advanced important reinterpretations of late. They now emphasize that the prospect of creating a united native Welsh polity under a single prince was no longer an idealist dream but a practical proposition. Indeed, during the decade 1267–77, it was briefly, if prematurely, realized. The shattering of that prospect — so recently glimpsed and even briefly realized — was thereby proportionately more traumatic. The Edwardian conquest was not just another and, as it proved, final onslaught against Wales; it involved the demolition of a new political vision. It was that which made it a national conquest and a national disaster.

The evidence for this reinterpretation comes from various directions. It has become increasingly clear that *Llywelyn ab Iorwerth*, Prince of Gwynedd, *c*.1199–1240, and his grandson, Llywelyn ap Gruffudd, 1247–82, strove with remarkable determination, clarity of objective and considerable success to convert the primacy of Gwynedd among the native dynasties into the leadership of a united native Wales whose status as a separate and unitary principality would be acknowledged by the English Crown (as indeed it was in the Treaty of Montgomery, 1267). They seized every opportunity to bring the other native rulers of Wales under their firm control and to weld *pura Wallia* — as the unconquered parts of Wales were called in contemporary documents — into an effective political unit. The obstacles that faced them were wellnigh insuperable, the time at their disposal short and their success only provisional and limited; but the tenacity with which they pursued their aims — in their own words to secure 'unity' and 'one peace and one war', to defend 'our principality' and its 'rights' and to reduce other native rulers to the status of 'Welsh barons of Wales' — was remarkable and revolutionary (Essay A). It is no wonder that Llywelyn ap Gruffudd was addressed by the poets as 'the true king of Wales' (*gwir frenin Cymru*) and 'as the man who was for Wales' (*gŵr oedd tros Gymru*). Such compliments were not mere poetic extravagance; they indicated that the nature of political ambitions, arguments and relationships within Wales and between Wales and England was changing profoundly.

A growing sense of the potential unity of Wales was, however, not merely a by-product of princely ambition; it drew also upon a heightened awareness of a common nationhood within Wales itself. Such an awareness expressed itself negatively in hatred for the English and for English settlers in Wales, 'the foreign alien-tongued people' (*estron genedl anghyfiaith*) as one poet contemptuously called it. Even official documents were driven to concede that 'the peoples of England and Wales have been at loggerheads for a long time'; in other words the tension between them was seen as national and popular, not merely as the result of the intransigence of individual princes. National pride and a sense of identity as a single people also had to them a positive dimension: the Welsh came to exult in their 'liberty' (as the Scots were to do later), their customs, their language and, above all, their laws. On the eve of the final catastrophe of December 1282 one of their spokesmen declared defiantly that the Welsh would never 'do *homage* to a stranger with whose language, customs and laws they are unfamiliar' (Source A.18). It is a statement which can be placed beside the Irish Remonstrance of 1317 and the Scottish Declaration of Arbroath of 1320 as one of the most dignified and eloquent defences of national self-determination in the Middle Ages. Nor were these mere words. Many Welshmen, it is true, fought in Edward I's armies in 1282–3 as they had done in those of other English kings and lords within and without Wales for generations; but what is truly astonishing is the wide degree of support — in geographical, social and regional terms — which the great revolt of 1282 came to enjoy. In the words of one distinguished historian it was truly 'a wide-spread popular rising of the Welsh'; its collapse, therefore, was a national defeat.

There was another sense in which the events of 1277–83 were different from earlier raids and conquests of parts of Wales. This was, and was meant to be, a final and complete conquest. The public statements of Edward I were suffused with an altogether new venom against the Welsh: they were 'a faithless people'; their rulers were 'a family of traitors'; it was time 'to put an end finally . . . to their malice'. In spite of the claim of one contemporary chronicler that the King was 'determined to exterminate the whole people of that nation', Edward I was bent not on genocide but on an irreversible conquest. His determination became obvious in the uncompromising position he adopted in final negotiations with Llywelyn in October to November 1282. Those negotiations, undertaken in spite of Edward I's better judgement, were conducted by John Pecham, Archbishop of Canterbury. Their failure served to convince Pecham that more than a military conquest was necessary in Wales; nothing less than a sustained campaign of clerical reform, moral regeneration and political re-education could achieve the integration of the Welsh fully into the Christian and civilized world of western Europe (Source D.21). It was in pursuit of that ambitious and unattainable programme that Pecham embarked on a great visitation of Welsh dioceses in the summer of 1284 and issued a battery of ecclesiastical recommendations (Essay D).

Later in the year Edward I himself went on a great triumphal progress through Wales, leaving Chester in late September and arriving at Chepstow on 17 December. Edward was intent not on moral crusade but on demonstrating to all and sundry — *Marcher lords* as well as native Welsh — that his victory was complete and utter and that ultimately his authority brooked no challenge in any part of Wales. He had already taken several notable steps to communicate that message clearly. He had held a great victory celebration, to which knights from Europe and England were invited, at Nefyn, one of the favourite residences of the princes of Gwynedd, in July 1284; he had commandeered Llywelyn's halls to his own use or had dismantled them; he appropriated the most valuable and potent symbols of Welsh princely independence — Llywelyn's coronet, the matrix of his seal, the jewel or crown of Arthur and, above all, the most cherished relic in Wales, the piece of the True Cross known as *Y Groes Naid* (just as he removed the Stone of Scone from Scotland in 1296). In the Statute of Wales he had annexed the conquered lands in Wales to his crown, though without integrating them fully into the body of the English state; and simultaneously he demoted the status of the country from a 'principality' to a mere 'land' (*terra*). Such were the acts of a king bent on the destruction of the identity of Wales. Henceforth a chasm had been officially opened in the memory and history of Wales between the period 'before' and 'after our peace proclaimed in Wales', as the royal documents put it. In that sense the Edwardian conquest of Wales was as definitive, complete, irreversible and traumatic as the Norman conquest of England.

Henceforth Welshmen had to learn to live with that reality (Essay E). For some the process of adjustment proved to be a painful one. A serious revolt in west Wales in 1287 showed that even Welsh leaders who had welcomed and co-operated with Edward I did not find it easy to live in the harsh and aggressive world of Edwardian governance. But it was the great revolt of 1294–5, sweeping the country from Anglesey to Glamorgan, which manifested the depth of resentment generated by the experience of conquest. The Welsh, like so many colonial peoples, had discovered a new unity under the experience of foreign rule. The revolt drew upon many individual and specific grievances — notably recent heavy taxation and the heavy-handed and arbitrary behaviour of English officials — but it was also nourished by two deeper and more generalized sentiments which run as a profound undercurrent throughout the history of post-conquest Wales. The one was a sense of being discriminated against in their own country, of being second-class, underprivileged citizens. Such a sentiment was explained by the attitudes of English officials and settlers in Wales — ranging from an arrogant and nervous condescension ('the Welsh' as one of them remarked in 1296, 'are Welsh, and you need to understand them properly' [Source B.24]) — to an aggressive cultivation of their legal position and commercial privileges, especially by the 'English *burgesses* of the English boroughs in Wales'. Such attitudes were officially entrenched by the fiercely discriminating measures introduced by Edward I in response to the revolt of 1294 (Source C.11). The other sentiment which characterized Welsh attitudes in the post-conquest period drew not on recent feelings of defeat and alienation but on a centuries-old mythology. It was their belief that a Messianic deliverer, a second Arthur, *y mab darogan* as he was called in Welsh, would come one day to rescue them from the yoke of Saxon servitude.

Powerful as are mythologies and prophecies, men cannot live everyday lives by them; they have to live in the present, not in the past or the future. So it was that the Welsh gradually came to terms with the experience of conquest. Some doubtless did so with more enthusiasm, good grace and success than others. The path to accommodation was eased when the English government and governors of Wales recognized that in the running of a conquered country, working with the grain of native society, winning over its leaders, listening to its grievances and forging ties of service and reward with it are ultimately more successful routes to contentment than military control and alien governance. It was this process of mutual adjustment and the appreciation by the Welsh of their own powerlessness against the might of the English kingdom which eventually ensured that, in spite of periodic scares and continuing suspicion of what contemporaries called the 'lightheadedness' (that is, the unreliability and volatility) of the Welsh, the Edwardian conquest of Wales remained virtually unchallenged for more than a century after the great revolt of 1294–5.

A momentous episode such as Edward I's conquest of Wales presents many problems to the historian. Two may be briefly broached here. The first is that of the nature of the sources at the historian's command. Our interpretation of the past is considerably shaped by the documentation through which our knowledge of the past is filtered to us. It is overwhelmingly through English administrative sources — that is, through the records of English kings and lords, composed according to contemporary formulae and written in Latin — that we study the impact of conquest on Wales. They give a limiting, even a distorting, view of the past. This is the common experience of conquered societies, for it is one of the consequences of conquest that the conqueror becomes the keeper of official record and authorized memory. One of the major redactions of the native Welsh chronicle, *Brut y Tywysogyon*, ends in 1282 and the others become highly episodic; it is as if the historiographical memory of the Welsh was snuffed out by the trauma of conquest. Likewise — and not surprisingly — the native court poetry tradition in Wales suffered a devastating blow with the conquest; it was only later in the fourteenth century that a revived and transformed poetic tradition took its place. This dearth of vernacular, native sources makes the individual and communal petitions submitted by Welshmen to the king and his lords (Sources E.2–4, E.11, E.17, E.21–2) all the more valuable to the historian, for they help to articulate the anxieties, frustrations and grievances of the Welsh in the years after the conquest. Just as it takes particular skills and insight to try to write recent history 'from below' (in other words to get at the outlook and aspirations of ordinary people), so it is only by the most sensitive and controlled use of historical imagination as well as documentation that we come to appreciate what the experience of conquest meant to the Welsh in the time of Edward I and how much it affected them.

The second challenge presented by the topic — as by any major historical issue, medieval or modern — is that of interpretation. Conflicting views are as much a part of history as they are a part of everyday life. Contemporary opinions of the conquest of Wales were as diverse as are modern ones. To one contemporary obituarist, Llywelyn ap Gruffudd was nothing less than the law and light of his people, 'a model for those of the future'; but it comes as no surprise that English commentators saw matters differently, characterizing Llywelyn as the epitome of perfidy and his brother as full of treason. Contemporary views of Edward I likewise were widely at variance with each other: one commentator saw him as treacherous and inconstant, while another referred to his 'never failing righteousness'; one impugned his motives by calling him 'the covetous king', but his victory in Wales earned him, from another later writer, the sobriquet, 'good King Edward, the Conqueror'. In modern memory likewise the reputation of both men varies widely: in Wales, especially from the nineteenth century, Llywelyn has been accorded the status of a national hero as *Y Llyw Olaf*, the Last Leader; but in England Edward I's reputation as one of the more effective and successful of medieval English kings remains unchallenged.

Such differences of opinion are only to be expected: after all, 1282, like 1536, is bound to be an evocative date for patriotic Welshmen as is, say, 1789 for Frenchmen. But such differences of opinion arise not only from national postures and convictions, past and present (just as other differences arise from political or ideological positions); they may also be generated, or made more acute, by genuine differences of interpretation of the historical evidence itself. Two instances of such shifts in interpretation, both of them arising out of recent scholarly work, may be mentioned here. The first relates to the character and motive of the two principal actors, Llywelyn ap Gruffudd and Edward I. Both have been the subject of considerable historical revision of late and in neither case is national animus the determinant of the historiographical shift of opinion. Thus it is Welsh, not English, historians who have recently called Llywelyn's behaviour and motives into question, accusing him of high-handedness towards his subjects and fellow native rulers, of over-ambition, or irresponsible stubbornness, and of fumbling his way to disaster. In short, was Llywelyn himself primarily responsible for bringing his own principality crashing around his ears? But simultaneously Edward I's own reputation and motivation, both in general and in particular with respect to Wales, have been seriously called into question. His protestations of good faith look unconvincing on closer inspection; his policies have been castigated for their 'masterfulness', 'moral shabbiness' and 'double dealing'; while his intervention in Wales and Scotland has been branded as 'a burst of imperialist activity'. Historians have no keys into the hearts and motives of men; but, as these revisionist interpretations of the characters and behaviour of Llywelyn and Edward suggest, they must for ever be trying to probe the springs of action and in so doing challenging existing historical interpretations.

Much the same may be said of a second area where historical emphasis has shifted of late, that of the conquest of Wales itself. On one level the conquest appears to be, and is, the most uncomplicated of events — a great military victory secured for the future by a massive programme of castle-building and by a comprehensive governmental and legal settlement. But was its impact as clear-cut and profound as the documents seem to suggest or as traumatic as the anguished cries of the poets proclaimed it to be? Above all, why did the final conquest take place in 1282–3? Was it — as has been argued regarding the First World War, for example — the result of a sequence of unforeseen accidents? Could Llywelyn and Edward have forged a tolerable *modus vivendi* in their relationships? Or were there deep structural reasons in the development of both countries and peoples and in their relationship with each other which made a denouement inevitable? Without in any way underestimating the importance of the personal and accidental, it is on these 'structural reasons' that recent historical interpretation of this period has concentrated. Welsh historians have drawn attention to the profound political and social changes which native-controlled Wales underwent in the thirteenth century and have wondered whether the pretensions of the princes of Gwynedd to the leadership of native Wales were ultimately compatible with the increasingly demanding and interventionist *feudal* subjection which the kings of England required of them. English historians for their part have underlined the important transformation which the kingdom of England experienced during the same period. Having lost most of its lands on the Continent between 1204 and 1259, the English monarchy became, for the first time since the Norman conquest, firmly England-based; it could now afford to turn its attention more closely to its other dominions (as it saw them) within Britain. This switch in direction was accompanied by a heightening of English national awareness, by a pride in the insularity and superiority of English common law, and by a remarkable growth in the maturity and efficacy of English administration and with it of concepts of metropolitan control, bureaucratic and legal uniformity, and clear lines of delegation and answerability. Such far-reaching changes prompt one to ask whether English royal government had grown to the point where not only the military conquest of Wales but also the effective governmental control of the country were possible. Was the conquest of Wales just part of the process of the growth of the English state? Was it but one chapter of the story whereby English 'super-overlordship' (as it has been called) of the British Isles was being transformed and intensified into direct rule? And was it likely that Scotland would be the next 'case for treatment'?

Questions like these cannot be readily, nor ever conclusively, answered. In history the best we can do is to travel hopefully. But it is by travelling hopefully rather than by standing still, by asking new questions, by posing new connections, by probing our sources in different ways and by recognizing their shortcomings that we advance and enrich our historical understanding. That is as true of episodes which are as distant in time and apparently cut-and-dried in their interpretation as Edward I's conquest of Wales as it is of more recent and better-documented topics.

Welsh Society and Native Power before Conquest

J. BEVERLEY SMITH

During the month of September 1267 Cardinal Ottobuono, the papal legate in England, issued at Shrewsbury a document which embodied the results of prolonged negotiations conducted between the *proctors* of Henry III of England and those A.1 of Llywelyn ap Gruffudd of Wales (A.1). Ottobuono commended a treaty which, he confidently hoped, would bring to an end the conflict for so long waged between the English and Welsh nations, but only ten years later the two nations were once more at war, and after only another five years a new conflict arose which was to be resolved by Edward I's conquest of Wales. The legate knew well enough the extent of the difficulties encountered during the course of the negotiations at Shrewsbury, but there were some grounds for his optimism. Henry III and the Lord Edward, heir to the throne of England, had consented to an agreement which, for the first time in history, stabilized the political situation in Wales in a manner acceptable to its rulers, and established a relationship with England acceptable to the rulers of both countries. The fragmentation of political power in Wales had long been the bane of the nation's history, and from the Norman period onward it had been exacerbated by the intervention of English kings and magnates. A wide area had been wrenched from Welsh control to form the March of Wales, itself a highly fragmented area, but no English king had been able to maintain stability in the area which remained under Welsh rule. This could only be achieved either by thorough conquest or by a decisive political initiative within Wales itself, and for a generation a measure of internal stability was achieved under the cohesive power of *Llywelyn ab Iorwerth* (Llywelyn the Great). But, to be made secure and permanent, the political order envisaged by Llywelyn had to be recognized by the English king and, as this involved a new concept of the relationship between the Crown and independent Wales, this recognition was denied him. It was Llywelyn ap Gruffudd's unique achievement that, by a new assertion of power which enabled him to surmount the adversities of the period following the death of his grandfather, he was able to secure that vital royal recognition. Ottobuono may not have been the only person of objective judgement who might have concluded that the proceedings finally enacted at the ford of Montgomery, four days after the promulgation of the historic agreement, when Llywelyn ap Gruffudd did *homage* to Henry III, completed a political settlement which could secure that permanent stability which had eluded Welsh and English rulers alike for so long.

In searching for an explanation for the collapse of the settlement of 1267 historians have inevitably looked to the personal proclivities of the two main protagonists, Edward I and Llywelyn ap Gruffudd, and the conflict waged ten years later has been seen as the outcome of their mutual antagonism. But before the relations of the two men are considered, we need to examine the nature of the power exercised by Llywelyn ap Gruffudd in that 'principality of Wales' whose existence was formally recognized by the Treaty of Montgomery. Llywelyn's power rested on the twin foundations indicated in the style which he had assumed upon the inauguration of the principality nine years earlier, and which eventually became an accepted part of English *Chancery* usage. He styled himself 'Prince of Wales and Lord of Snowdon'. Initially sharing the rule of Snowdonia or Gwynedd Uwch Conwy (the land lying west of the Conwy and including Anglesey) with his elder brother Owain ap Gruffudd, Llywelyn had asserted complete control in 1255. In that year he withstood an attempt on the part of his younger brother, *Dafydd ap Gruffudd*, with Owain's support, to partition the narrow territory between the three of them. More than a triumph in a fraternal conflict, Llywelyn's decisive action at Bryn Derwin enabled him to withstand Henry III's attempt to promote the disintegration of Gwynedd whereby he insisted on an interpretation of Welsh inheritance custom which required that a territory should be shared among a ruler's sons. With four brothers to share Snowdonia (Rhodri ap Gruffudd was still to be provided for) the prospect for the monarchy was distinctly encouraging. For, if military conquest of Snowdonia had been beyond his capability, Henry had already been able to take possession of that part of Gwynedd which lay east of the Conwy (Perfeddwlad or the Four Cantrefs) and he could now look forward to an early partition of Snowdonia into four portions, a division which would greatly facilitate the extension of royal influence into the very heartland of Welsh resistance. He was foiled by the singular determination of Llywelyn ap Gruffudd

A.2   to prevent the fragmentation of Gwynedd (A.2). A year later the King lost control of Perfeddwlad when, in a forceful movement seen at the time as a campaign waged to liberate the people from the oppression which they had endured under the officers of the Lord Edward, to whom the King had entrusted the area, Llywelyn took possession of and established a dominion

A.3   extending from the Dyfi to the Dee (A.3).

Llywelyn was now 'Lord of Snowdon' in the fullest sense. He then moved swiftly to establish a still broader supremacy, but if his initial assertion of power in Powys and Deheubarth came by dint of military force, the Prince's enduring authority in these areas would rest upon the nexus which he established with each of the lords of these areas who acknowledged not simply his leadership in war but his lordship over them. Each one recognized Llywelyn's lordship by doing *homage* to him and swearing an oath of *fealty*, and thereupon lord and *vassal* entered into a set of mutual engagements specified in a document to which each of them put his seal. The text of an agreement made between Llywelyn and a late adherent, Gruffudd ap Gwen-

A.4   wynwyn, lord of Powys Wenwynwyn, survives (A.4); it consists, first, of a brief record of the fact that Gruffudd did *homage* and swore upon holy relics to be faithful to his lord, Llywelyn, and that Llywelyn thereupon granted him his lands. Secondly the document describes, at much greater length, the obligations to one another which lord and *vassal* recognized and, though these were a particular reflection of the agreements made between those two men, it is certain that comparable agreements were made between Llywelyn and each of those who recognized his lordship. It was by means of those agreements that he became 'Prince of Wales'. The power of Llywelyn therefore rested in part upon his ability to retain the fidelity of the community of Gwynedd, which he ruled directly as territorial lord, and partly upon his capacity to retain the allegiance of those barons of Powys and Deheubarth with whom he had established a contractual relationship and who, with their prince, formed the political community of the principality of Wales. With some barons, such as Maredudd ab Owain of Ceredigion and Gruffudd ap Madog of Powys Fadog, he established a stable relationship; with others, such as Gruffudd ap Gwenwynwyn and *Maredudd ap Rhys Gryg* of Ystrad Tywi, no enduring relationship proved possible, and the judicial processes to which these princes were subject on account of their infidelity serve both to demonstrate the strength of Llywelyn's jurisdiction and to indicate the extent to which the security of the principality depended upon the wholehearted commitment of the barons of Wales to the new polity. It would take many years, perhaps several generations, for a prince of Wales to extend over the whole of the principality a territorial lordship comparable to that which he exercised in Gwynedd. In the meantime the prince had to deal with men who were, no less than himself, descendants of royal figures who had hitherto acknowledged no superior lordship other than that of the king of England. If, for any reason, they were disillusioned with their lot in the principality of Wales they would be liable to revert to their traditional *fealty* to the king of England, and Llywelyn had precious little time to weld the principality into a political structure within which he could exercise those judicial, military and financial powers which were the normal attributes of medieval governance. He recognized that it was essential to insulate his principality against intervention on the part of the English Crown, but he knew that he would be better able to do so if he secured the King's formal recognition of what he had achieved within Wales. This was certainly his dominant concern in the period following his initial assertion of power over the provinces of independent Wales and eventually, by the key clause of the Treaty of

Montgomery, he was formally conceded the *homage* and *fealty* of all the Welsh barons of Wales, with the single exception of *Maredudd ap Rhys Gryg* (A.5). It was this historic change in the political order within Wales, and hence in its relationship with England, that Cardinal Ottobuono commended in the late summer of 1267.

It would not be fair to say that the years immediately following the making of the settlement were unpropitious, nor would it be true to say that the situation was fundamentally and immediately affected by the accession of Edward I in 1272. After 1267 Edward, anxious to put the whole experience of the *barons' wars* behind him, seemed prepared to set aside the disagreeable memory of Llywelyn's involvement with *Simon de Montfort* and to countenance those advances into the March which the Prince had made at the expense of Crown and *Marcher lord* alike. The Prince of Wales and the heir to the throne of England showed that they were capable of conducting purposeful negotiations, and Henry III commended Llywelyn for his accommodating attitude at a particularly encouraging meeting with Edward at the ford of Montgomery in 1269. The record of the exchanges between the two men suggests very strongly that Llywelyn would have been troubled, rather than relieved, by the knowledge that Edward planned to leave the realm upon a crusade to the Holy Land, realizing that his prolonged absence would greatly hamper meaningful discussion of important issues. He was no doubt fearful, too, of the influences which might now be exerted upon the ageing King, particularly that of *Roger Mortimer*, the baron whom the Prince recognized as his main adversary among the Marchers. Edward left the realm in the summer of 1270 and did not return for four years. Not all the problems which had accumulated by his return had their origin in the period of his absence, for a number of difficulties had already arisen in March 1270. One of the most serious arose from a tendentious interpretation of the Treaty of Montgomery by which Llywelyn endeavoured to claim as 'a Welsh baron of Wales' the *homage* of Gruffudd ap Rhys of Senghennydd, a *mesne tenant* of *Gilbert de Clare* in the lordship of Glamorgan. But the hardening of attitudes, revealed on all sides within weeks of Edward's departure, and the convergence of interest which brought *Clare* and *Mortimer* to surmount their mutual antipathy, marked an intensification of the conflict in the March which was to have dire consequences for Llywelyn's position in several of the areas conceded to him in 1267. By the time Edward returned to England (as its king since the death of Henry III in November 1272), his regents had a great deal to relate, and we may safely assume that he was informed in detail of the Prince's relations, not only with the administration which had been maintained in the king's name during his absence, but with the Marchers, the barons of his principality, his younger brother *Dafydd ap Gruffudd* and, perhaps, with the community of his own territorial lordship in Gwynedd. The issues raised by these relations are often intertwined with one another but each may be noticed in turn.

Llywelyn's power had extended beyond the confines of the three provinces of Gwynedd, Powys and Deheubarth into several areas of the March, and his appropriation of lordships such as Gwerthrynion, Elfael, Brecon and Maelienydd had meant the disinheritance of Marcher magnates who had hitherto been firmly entrenched in those areas. In each of these lordships, as in the former royal lordship of Builth, his power rested, not upon a relationship with a single *mesne lord*, but with an entire community. These were largely Welsh communities and several of them had adhered to him during the offensives which had carried him into the area, but each community included men with close links to the Marcher families who had previously ruled those areas, and there is evidence that Llywelyn was by no means certain of the fidelity of some of these influential persons. In Brecon, for instance, he faced a dual problem. First, *Humphrey de Bohun*, heir to the expropriated lord, endeavoured to reassert himself. He was encouraged by *Roger Mortimer*, who acted not only in the role of sympathetic fellow-Marcher with a comparable wish to reassert his hold on Gwerthrynion and Maelienydd but, much more seriously, in his capacity as a regent of the realm. A letter addressed to him by two clerical colleagues in the royal administration, written in reply to his inquiry, reveals *Mortimer*'s wish to establish that it would be legitimate to deploy royal forces to support *Bohun* in his bid to recover A.6   Brecon (A.6). It reflects the influence which *Mortimer* exerted at the centre of affairs, a matter to which Llywelyn himself alludes in his response to a letter which he received from the royal *Chancery*; written in the king's name but effectively dictated by *Mortimer*, the letter ordered him to cease work at Dolforwyn, a castle he was building in the lordship of Cydewain, conceded to

A.7   him in 1267 (A.7). But, secondly, *Bohun*'s prospects of recovering Brecon were enhanced, not only by expectation of royal support, but by an ominous lack of fidelity among Llywelyn's tenants in the lordship. It is revealed as early as 1271 in his attempt to make certain of the loyalty of a tenant named Meurig ap Llywelyn, by first taking a hostage for his allegiance and then releasing the hostage in return for a new guarantee of fidelity

A.8   (A.8). In this and similar cases Llywelyn's efforts were in vain, and he was eventually confronted, not simply with an external attack by a Marcher power acting with royal support, but with the disintegration of his authority within the area itself as persons of consequence in the community reverted to their allegiance to the *Marcher lords*.

These were strategic areas, but they lay beyond the confines of the three historical provinces upon which the principality was founded, and the retention of the outlying areas would not be essential to the security of the principality if the Prince were certain of the allegiance of the lords of Powys and Deheubarth. But he had never been quite certain of his position in these territories. The single exception of *Maredudd ap Rhys Gryg* of Ystrad Tywi from among the barons of Wales whose *homage* was conceded to Llywelyn in 1267 reflects the turbulent relationship between the Prince and this powerful figure. *Maredudd*'s early adherence had been quickly followed by a defection, a reconciliation and a second defection which clearly illustrates the difficulty which Llywelyn could face in endeavouring to reconcile the interests of his barons with his vision of a united Welsh dominion. The agreement made between them in 1261, when a new attempt at reconciliation was made, reflects the lack

A.9   of trust between them (A.9), and in the critical summer of 1277 it was *Maredudd*'s son, *Rhys ap Maredudd*, who was the first baron of Deheubarth to succumb to the entreaties of a King who knew that, without any great expenditure upon military forces, he could exploit the dynastic contentions among the princes of the provinces. *Rhys ap Maredudd*'s defection was, in fact, to lead to a complete collapse of Llywelyn's position as other members of the dynasty of Deheubarth came to realize that they had need to salvage their baronies. There was a comparable disintegration of the Prince's power in Powys. Gruffudd ap Gwenwynwyn, whose agreement with Llywelyn provides a rare exemplar of a concord between prince and baron, is unlikely ever to have enthused over his membership of the Welsh political community. A person with an estate located upon an exposed front of the principality and having close connections with his peers of the English nobility among whom he had been reared, it might have been expected that Gruffudd would revert to the king's *fealty* sooner or later. But in 1274 he chose not to depart but to join *Dafydd ap Gruffudd* in a conspiracy to kill Llywelyn and raise the younger brother to the princedom. The coup was foiled and the conspirators eventually fled to England but it is significant that initially they had planned, not a flight from the principality, but rebellion. The judicial process by which, in the interval between conspiracy and flight, Llywelyn secured Gruffudd's conviction for infidelity demonstrates his princely power, but at the same time it reveals the difficulties which he faced in endeavouring to retain the confidence of men who knew that, if they were ever driven to extremity, they would be able to turn to the alternative authority of a protective monarch (A.10).

A.10

The conspiracy, a crucial occurrence in the train of events in the period immediately preceding the King's return to England, provides a link between the problem of baronial fidelity and the difficulties within the dynasty of Gwynedd. These, seemingly resolved at Bryn Derwin, were kept alive by the fervid ambition of *Dafydd ap Gruffudd*, and threatened to undermine Llywelyn's position even as Lord of Snowdon. The clause in the Treaty of Montgomery which deals with the provision to be made for Dafydd vindicates the Prince's interpretation of Welsh dynastic custom (A.11). The clause, 'specially ordained' though it might be, did no more than specify that Dafydd should receive an estate within his brother's dominion; the King would be informed of the provision made, but Dafydd's lot would be determined within Llywelyn's jurisdiction. After a second

A.11

defection at the end of 1274 Dafydd participated in the growing harassment of Llywelyn from the security of Edward's protection and, when the King came to terms with Llywelyn in 1277, the clause concerning Dafydd provides a poignant reflection of Llywelyn's changed circumstances. He had now to recognize the hereditary right of his brother to his share of the patrimony in Snowdonia itself, and it was only by the King's grace that he was able to retain possession, for his lifetime, of

A.12 the portion which belonged to Dafydd (A.12). The younger brother's tenacity ensured that, though Owain was effectively eliminated by perpetual imprisonment and Rhodri presented no known challenge, the dynastic problems were to haunt the Prince of Wales and give the King a divisive instrument which he used with devastating dexterity.

The fact that Dafydd, rather than defect a second time, chose to conspire to replace Llywelyn in 1274 prompts the question whether he had reason at that stage to believe that circumstances in Gwynedd were propitious for rebellion. As a baron of Gwynedd, holding an extensive estate in Perfeddwlad, Dafydd had a base from which he could launch a challenge to Llywelyn's authority, but he may have had reason to believe that an initiative on his part might win broader support. It seems fair to conclude that Llywelyn had incurred heavy financial liabilities, even though the only charge which may be quantified is the *indemnity* which he owed to the King for the Treaty of Montgomery and which was paid in annual instalments. He fell into arrears with his payments before the death of Henry III and his failure to pay may have been due, not to any decision to withhold delivery on an issue of principle, but simply to the fact that he found it difficult to raise the money. The brave words of a letter in which he declared that the money was ready for delivery, if only the King compelled the *Marchers* to cease their attacks upon him, come at a late date, after some years in which he had dispatched evasive missives and made

A.13 piecemeal deliveries to the royal *Exchequer* (A.13). Llywelyn undoubtedly faced other liabilities, too, more especially the costs of building and maintaining castles (notably the building of Dolforwyn) and of continuing conflict in the March, and these charges were borne essentially by the community of his territorial lordship in Gwynedd. There appears to be no evidence that the lords of Powys and Deheubarth contributed to his coffers, and it is not unlikely that the income which accrued to him for his lordships in the March was entirely expended on the defence and the internal security of those areas. There is, in fact, much to suggest that the community of Gwynedd was subjected to heavy financial pressure in the period leading up to the war of 1277; evidence from the period after Llywelyn's death provides a graphic account of the breaches of custom and the extractive practices which the community endured in these critical years, and it is conceivable that the Prince's harsh dealings with his own tenants created A.14   deep resentment (A.14). To what extent these pressures undermined his support in his own dominions is impossible to tell. We know that, for whatever reason, some key members of the community defected to the King during the course of the conflict, men such as *Rhys ap Gruffudd* and Gruffudd ap Iorwerth, who represented powerful lineages. But the Prince's problems may have involved more than a desertion on the part of some members of the élite of his community, however disturbing their inconstancy may have been. His ultimate submission to the King in 1277 may reflect the power of men of substance, who may have remained loyal, but who may have forced the Prince to acknowledge that he had driven his people to the utmost limits of their endurance.

There were indications that Llywelyn faced difficulties within the various parts of his principality even before Edward returned to his kingdom, and the King would undoubtedly have taken these into account in making decisions on the matters which concerned him directly. Edward insisted upon two cardinal matters: that the Prince should fulfil his obligations as a *vassal* by doing *homage* and *fealty*, and that he should fulfil his financial obligations under the Treaty of Montgomery. He brought matters to a head when he summoned Llywelyn to Chester in the summer of 1275. Llywelyn, less concerned now with the continuing conflict in the March than with the issues which had arisen between the King and himself, expressed his anger that those who had conspired to kill him found refuge in England and were even allowed to harass him from the safety of

Idealized sculpture of Llywelyn ap Gruffudd in Cardiff City Hall. (*Source: Cardiff City Council.*)

the King's protection. King and prince hovered upon the frontier of the principality, within a few miles of one another, but neither felt able to yield on the crucial issues and they

A.15   eventually went their separate ways (A.15). Before the year was out Edward secured full confirmation of a suspicion which he had probably harboured of Llywelyn even before he summoned him to Chester, a factor which intensified the contention between them still further.

This was Llywelyn's decision to marry Eleanor de Montfort, daughter of the baronial leader who had plunged England into civil war in the previous reign. At the end of 1275 Eleanor was captured at sea while making her way from her refuge at the priory of Montargis in France to join Llywelyn, to whom she had already been married by proxy. In forceful language Edward denounced the machinations of those who sought to revive the turmoil which England had endured in the time of

A.16   *Simon de Montfort* (A.16); his letters to the papacy rejected every plea for Eleanor's release from detention and denounced the intransigence of a prince who was no more than 'one of the greatest among the other magnates of my kingdom'.

Llywelyn never denied that he held his principality under the

A.6   King's authority (A.6). He consistently stressed his inherent rights, derived from his predecessors, the kings and princes of his dynasty, but from the outset he had sought to establish a nexus with the Crown and saw royal recognition as a key factor in the stabilization of his power. Edward naturally preferred to concentrate upon Llywelyn's obligations as a *tenant-in-chief* and declared his duty to apply his corrective hand to a contumacious *vassal*. He registered his success in doing so in the Treaty of Aberconwy in 1277, though the text makes no mention of the dismembering of the principality of Wales, and the structure by which Llywelyn had exercised political power passed into

A.17   oblivion without any formal abrogation (A.17). The treaty was concerned very largely with Gwynedd, and Llywelyn, Prince of Wales though he might still be in name, was confined to Snowdonia and Anglesey. Thereafter there were two matters which may have concerned him more than any others. On the one hand he hoped for a male heir through whom his thwarted aspirations might yet find fulfilment. On the other hand he used the debate on the issue of Welsh law (originating in an argument as to which law should be used in his dispute with Gruffudd ap Gwenwynwyn over possession of the land of Arwystli) to propound ideas of nationhood which were potentially of profound significance. These ideas struck a chord with princes who nursed their own resentments against the King; Llywelyn, though deprived of the instruments of political power which he had previously enjoyed, became a focus for the frustrations and aspirations of members of princely dynasties who had not been conspicuous for their constancy in years gone by. Yet it is unlikely that the inspiration for rebellion came from Llywelyn. He had every reason to hold his hand awhile, but for the lords of Powys and Deheubarth and for the community of the Perfeddwlad, and for those other areas immediately subject to royal administration, time was running out. Reluctantly, perhaps, Llywelyn committed himself to a new conflict not of his making and brought to the disparate endeavours of desperate men the sustaining power for which his last letters, written within a few weeks of his death, provide an eloquent

A.18   remembrance (A.18). It was an emotive force which Edward was able to confront with the relentless coercive power with which he waged his just war. It was only after the Prince's death and the cessation of hostilities a few months later that Edward I, taking possession of the Prince's coronet and of the sacred relic of the *Croes Naid*, made a tacit acknowledgement of their inherent royal right which had provided the creative force of the political expression of medieval Welsh nationhood.

Sources

A.1   God, creator of all, who in a world of such diversity and contradiction, established the earth in such harmony so that all things have their boundaries and exist by an established law, sometimes through his mysterious judgement permits the human race, which represents the image of the world, to be troubled by the discords of wars, and then by his will restores it to the unity of peace. The people of England and Wales have quarrelled for a long time, perhaps both suffering in turn, and have been afflicted by many troubles and wars. God has looked upon them with a merciful eye and wishing in these days to put an end to their sufferings, has led them through his goodness to agreement. The lord Henry, illustrious king of England, and the noble Llywelyn ap Gruffudd have come to peace and agreement, rising above all the quarrels and disagreements which formerly existed between them and the wrongs and injuries which are said to have arisen therefrom . . . All complaints, offences, wrongs, transgressions and injuries perpetrated by Llywelyn and his men against the king and his tenants, and likewise those committed against Llywelyn and his people by the king's men and tenants are fully and mutually forgiven and pardoned.

(25 and 29 September 1267. Treaty of Montgomery. Agreement between King Henry III and Prince Llywelyn ap Gruffudd was announced by Cardinal Ottobuono at Shrewsbury on 25 September; the treaty was sealed at Montgomery, where Llywelyn did homage to Henry on 29 September. J. G. Edwards, *Littere Wallie*, Cardiff, 1940, pp. 1–4.)

A.2   In those days great strife was bred at the instigation of the Devil between the sons of Gruffudd ap Llywelyn, namely Owain Goch and Dafydd, on the one side, and Llywelyn, on the other side. And then Llywelyn and his men, trusting in God, awaited unafraid on Bryn Derwin the fierce coming of his brothers, and a mighty host along with them. And before the end of one hour Owain Goch was captured and Dafydd fled, after many of his host had been slain and others been captured and the remainder had fled. And then Owain was imprisoned, and Llywelyn gained possession of the territory of Owain and Dafydd without opposition to him.

(1255. T. Jones (ed.), *Brut y Tywysogyon or The Chronicle of the Princes, Red Book of Hergest Version*, Cardiff, 1955, p. 247.)

A.3   The following year Edward, son of king Henry, earl of Chester, came to survey his castles and his lands in Gwynedd. And then the magnates of Wales, despoiled of their liberty and reduced to bondage, came to Llywelyn ap Gruffudd and mournfully made known to him that they preferred to be slain in battle for their liberty than to suffer themselves to be trampled upon in bondage by men alien to them. And Llywelyn was moved by their tears, and at their persuasion and by their counsel he made for Perfeddwlad and gained possession of it all within the week.

(1256. Jones, *Brut y Tywysogyon, Red Book of Hergest Version*, p.247.)

A.4   This is the final concord made on the Vigil of St Lucy the Virgin at Ystumanner between the lord Llywelyn ap Gruffudd, prince of Wales, on the one part, and the lord Gruffudd ap Gwenwynwyn, on the other, namely, that the lord Gruffudd of his free will did *homage* for himself and his heirs and, touching holy objects, swore *fealty* to the lord Llywelyn and his heirs . . . In return for his *homage* and *fealty* Llywelyn granted and restored to Gruffudd all his lands and possessions . . . Gruffudd and his heirs shall hold and possess their lands by their *metes and bounds* from the lord Llywelyn and his heirs forever by hereditary right . . . If war or attack is waged upon the land of Gruffudd, and Llywelyn is not troubled by war or attack at that time, Llywelyn shall aid the lord Gruffudd before all his other allies, if his need is the greater. If it were to happen that Gruffudd should lose his castle of Pool in war . . . Llywelyn shall provide Gruffudd with another castle where he could keep his possessions and family safely until he should recover his castle. The lord Gruffudd is bound to come with the lord Llywelyn upon campaign whenever he is required to do so unless a hostile invasion of his land then manifestly threatens. Each of the lords Llywelyn and Gruffudd are bound together to be of one war and one peace, and neither will enter into any alliance without the other . . . For the full faith and security of these agreements Llywelyn and Gruffudd put themselves and their lands under the jurisdiction of the bishops of Bangor and St Asaph and the abbots of Aberconwy and Pool . . . so that jointly and individually they may pronounce sentence of *excommunication* upon the persons of Llywelyn and Gruffudd and their heirs and *interdict* upon their lands if they presume to act contrary to any of the articles of agreement.

(12 December 1274. Agreement between Llywelyn ap Gruffudd, Prince of Wales and Gruffudd ap Gwenwynwyn, lord of Powys Wenwynwyn, at Ystumanner in Meirionnydd. Edwards, *Littere Wallie*, pp.77–80.)

A.5   The lord king, wishing to exalt the person of Llywelyn and to honour those who shall succeed him by hereditary right, entirely of his liberality and grace, and by the assent of the lord Edward, his first-born son, gives and grants to Llywelyn and his heirs the principality of Wales, so that Llywelyn and his heirs shall be called and be princes of Wales, and moreover [have] the *fealty* and *homage* of all the Welsh barons of Wales, so that the said barons shall hold their lands in chief from the prince and his heirs, except the *homage* of the noble man Maredudd ap Rhys, whose *homage* and lordship the king retains for himself and his heirs.

(25–9 September 1267. Treaty of Montgomery. Edwards, *Littere Wallie*, pp.1–4.)

A.6   We have received your letters describing how the Welsh have recently plundered and burned *Humphrey de Bohun*'s land of Brecon and, in response to your wish, we have examined the treaty negotiated between King Henry and Llywelyn ap Gruffudd . . . We do not consider it expedient to defend the land against Llywelyn by the mandate and power of the king, for it is clear that that would infringe the treaty . . . but as Llywelyn, neither when the treaty was made nor subsequently, had possession of the castles of the said Humphrey, it is very expedient to defend them and give effective assistance for the defence.

(Probably early in 1273. Robert Burnell, a regent of the realm, and Walter Merton, the Chancellor, to Roger Mortimer, a regent. J. G. Edwards, *Calendar of Ancient Correspondence concerning Wales*, Cardiff, 1935, pp.109–10.)

A.7   We have received the letter written in your name forbidding us to construct a castle on our own land near Abermiwl or to establish a town or market there. We are certain that the letter was not issued with your knowledge, and that if you were present in your kingdom such an order would not be issued from your *chancery*. For you know that the rights of our principality are entirely separate from the rights of your kingdom, though we hold our principality under your royal power . . . We pray you not to listen to those who try to inflame your mind against us.

(11 July 1273. Llywelyn ap Gruffudd, Prince of Wales and Lord of Snowdon, at Dinorben, to Edward I, concerning the castle of Dolforwyn in Cydewain; when the letter was written Edward was in Savoy and he did not reach England until August 1274. Edwards, *Calendar of Ancient Correspondence*, p.86.)

A.8   Know that we [Meurig ap Llywelyn], for the release of our hostage whom we gave to our lord Llywelyn, prince of Wales and lord of Snowdon, for our constant adherence to the *fealty* and *homage* which we did to him, have given the underwritten sureties that, upon any day which the lord Llywelyn may wish, we shall hand over the hostage, to be held in custody as he is held at present. If we do not restore the hostage or if we withdraw from the *homage* and *fealty* of the prince, the sureties shall remain pledged to the prince on our behalf for one hundred marks, namely Hywel ap Rhys Gryg, Trahaearn ap Cadwgan . . . Maredudd ap Cynwrig. We also place ourselves under the jurisdiction of the lord bishop of St Davids . . . that he may pronounce sentence of *excommunication* upon our person if we presume to contravene this writing.

(7 November 1271. Charter, written at Rhyd-y-briw in the lordship of Brecon, by which Meurig ap Llywelyn pledged his fealty to Prince Llywelyn. Edwards, *Littere Wallie*, p.126. A mark was equivalent to two-thirds of a pound sterling, 13s.4d.)

A.9   The lord Llywelyn receives Maredudd into his peace and goodwill . . . [and] . . . restores to him all the lands which were in his possession when he last withdrew from his unity . . .

Maredudd ap Rhys is bound to come with all his might to do his service and duty to Llywelyn in person, for the harassing and suppressing of Llywelyn's enemies in Deheubarth whenever and wherever there is need, without feigning, cavilling, excusing or objecting . . . when Maredudd is required by the lord Llywelyn to do so. He shall give twenty-four hostages from among the sons of the noblemen of his land whom Llywelyn shall choose. If Maredudd presumes to act contrary to the present agreement . . . he shall forfeit . . . every right and claim to his inheritance in Deheubarth. Furthermore if Maredudd presumes to act in a manner contrary to what is agreed, he shall place himself under the jurisdiction of the lords bishops of Bangor and St Asaph . . . so that they shall pronounce sentence of *excommunication* upon his person and his household and followers.

(6 December 1261. Agreement, made at Coleshill, between Llywelyn ap Gruffudd and Maredudd ap Rhys, following Maredudd's release from prison after his second defection from Llywelyn. Edwards, *Littere Wallie*, pp.104–5.)

A.10 The lord Gruffudd [ap Gwenwynwyn] and his son Owain confessed that they had breached the *fealty* due to the lord prince and . . . the judges decided that the persons of the lord Gruffudd and his son, and their lands and possessions, should be placed in the grace and will of the lord prince . . . Gruffudd acknowledged that he had seriously transgressed against the prince and, humbly prostrating himself on bended knee at the feet of the lord prince, prayed this mercy of him, that the prince would grant him from among his hereditary lands Y Teirswydd, Caereinion, Cyfeiliog from Arwystli to the Dyfi, Mawddwy and Mochnant Uwch Rhaeadr . . . The lord prince granted these lands to him and his heirs provided that the lord Gruffudd and his heirs shall remain faithful to him while they live and that . . . Owain shall be given as a hostage for the fidelity of his father . . . And the lord prince shall receive the *homage* of twenty-five men chosen from Gruffudd's lands who shall swear upon holy relics that they will remain faithful to the prince if Gruffudd manifestly transgresses, or if he be convicted of any evident transgression the said twenty-five men, forsaking altogether their *homage* and *fealty* to him, shall thereafter, with his consent, be inseparably united with the lord prince.

(17 April 1274. Record of a legal process brought by Llywelyn ap Gruffudd against Gruffudd ap Gwenwynwyn before a board of arbitrators agreed by both parties at 'Bachyrannelau in Cydewain', probably Dolforwyn. Edwards, *Littere Wallie*, pp. 108–10.)

A.11   Concerning Dafydd, brother of Llywelyn, it is specially ordained that Llywelyn shall restore to him the whole land which Dafydd held before he withdrew from him and adhered to the king, and if Dafydd is not satisfied additional provision shall be made as Gruffudd ap Gwenwynwyn, Gruffudd ap Madog, Hywel ap Madog, Owain ap Bleddwyn and Tudur ab Ednyfed shall in good faith ordain; . . . if Dafydd remains unsatisfied he shall ask for what he desires and justice shall be done to him according to the laws and customs of Wales in the presence of one or two who shall inform the king what justice was done to him and how it was done; and all this shall be provided and done for Dafydd before next Christmas, notwithstanding any obstacle or delay or difficulty.

(25–9 September 1267. Treaty of Montgomery. Edwards, *Littere Wallie*, pp. 1–4.)

A.12   The lord king, entirely of his grace, concedes and confirms to prince Llywelyn for his lifetime the whole land which is due to Dafydd his brother by hereditary right, and the lord king will make adequate recompense elsewhere for Llywelyn's lifetime and, either upon the death of Llywelyn or Dafydd, the land given to Dafydd in recompense shall freely be restored to the king and his heirs.

(9 November 1277. Treaty of Aberconwy. Edwards, *Littere Wallie*, pp. 118–22.)

A.13   The money which we are bound to pay to you for the peace which was made between the late King Henry and ourselves is ready to be paid to your attorneys, provided that you fulfil in respect to ourselves what ought to be done according to the terms of the peace. We therefore ask you to compel the earl of Gloucester, *Humphrey de Bohun* and the rest of the Marchers to restore to us the lands which they unjustly occupied and more unjustly detain, and we shall immediately pay the money to you.

(Probably 26 February 1274. Llywelyn ap Gruffudd, at Cricieth, to Edward I. Edwards, *Calendar of Ancient Correspondence*, pp.92–3.)

A.14   The prince used to take townships for his own use, or to grant them to others in return for services, but the burden of that township remained upon the community or upon other townships, and it is a great wrong to place the burden of one township upon another. The prince took great and small lands without the consent of the heirs and placed his cattle-pastures and plough lands there, and took profit from land which was sold, something which no other prince did except him alone . . . The prince frequently waged war against you, lord king, without consulting his people and without seeking and obtaining their agreement, and when, in the course of time, peace was made between you and him he made his men pay three pence a year for every great beast, yet he was not willing to pay anything from his treasure deposited at Dolwyddelan and elsewhere . . . In the time of Llywelyn the measure of wine, corn and beer was increased . . . The prince made the noblemen of Meirionnydd bear the cost of horses to carry burdens and perform his duties, and demanded pasture for other horses, something which had never occurred before his time. In Arfon, where before the time of the prince there were only one court-house, one *bailiff* and two servants, now they are doubled. There the prince made *villeins* out of noblemen . . . Never in the past have these or similar wrongs been attempted or contemplated by any prince or king except by the said prince Llywelyn. For this reason the people pray God that remedy may be brought against such matters.

(2 August 1283. Complaints levied against Llywelyn ap Gruffudd by representatives of the community of Gwynedd

before Anian, Bishop of Bangor, at Nancall in Arfon. Llinos Beverley Smith, 'The Gravamina of the Community of Gwynedd against Llywelyn ap Gruffudd', *Bulletin of the Board of Celtic Studies*, XXXI, 1984, pp.173–6.)

A.15   In that year, about the feast of Mary in September, king Edward came from London to Chester, and he summoned to him prince Llywelyn to do him *homage*. And the prince in turn summoned to him all the barons of Wales, and by common counsel he did not go to the king because the king maintained his fugitives, namely *Dafydd ap Gruffudd* and Gruffudd ap Gwenwynwyn. And for that reason the king returned enraged to England, and Llywelyn returned to Wales.

(1275. Jones, *Brut y Tywysogyon*, p.263.)

A.16   We do not believe that you have forgotten how *Simon de Montfort* and all his family fought with all their strength against King Henry, our father, and ourselves and our men . . . Eleanor, his daughter, following the counsel of her relatives and friends, of whom there are many in our kingdom, arranged to marry the prince of Wales, believing, though wrongly, that through a marriage to the prince she could, by his power, spread abroad against us in the fullness of time the old seed of malice which her father had conceived, and which she could not spread about on her own. But divine providence, which is infallible in its disposition, returned her to us unexpectedly, confounded by her own error . . . We are justly angered against her and her fellow conspirators, and no less so against two brothers of the *Dominican* order, noblemen of Welsh birth, found and held in her company, since the said stratagems and schemes are said to have been due to their planning and ingenuity . . . Since we do not believe that this marriage was contracted without the convenience and consultation of many people, we ask as a particular favour that you in your wisdom carefully question the said brothers about this.

(Early 1276. Edward I to Robert Kilwardby, Archbishop of Canterbury, following the capture of Eleanor de Montfort at sea. N. Denholm-Young, *The Liber Epistolaris of Richard de Bury*, no.85, London, 1950.)

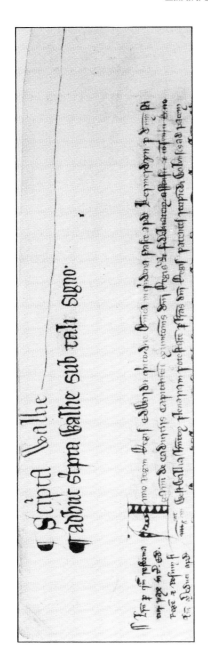

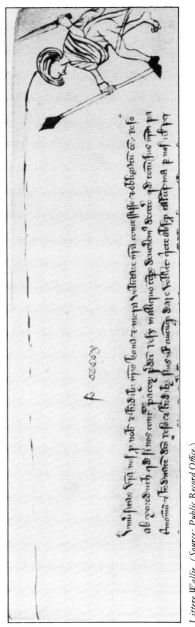

Littere Wallie. (Source: Public Record Office.)

A.17   Llywelyn submits himself to the will and mercy of the lord king and for the disobedience, damages and injuries done to the king and his men he gives, to have his peace, fifty thousand marks sterling, and prays the king's grace and mercy in respect of that sum. Llywelyn grants . . . to the king of England and his heirs, for himself and his heirs fully and without reservation, the Four *Cantreds* . . . along with all the lands which the lord king captured . . . except the land of Anglesey . . . Llywelyn shall come to Rhuddlan to swear an oath of *fealty* to the lord king, and before he comes to the king's presence he shall receive the blessing of *absolution* and the *interdict* of his land shall be lifted . . . The prince . . . gives the lord king ten hostages from among the noblemen of his land whom he can find without compulsion of imprisonment or disinheritance . . . the prince grants that he and those of his council shall immediately swear, and twenty men from each *cantref* in his lands elected before the prince's officers by faithful men of the king sent there each year shall likewise swear, year by year before the said faithful men of the king, that they will observe these agreements as fully as lies in their power and will secure the prince's observance, and, if the prince in any way contravenes and does not make amends in reasonable time, they will then withdraw from the *fealty*, *homage*, lordship and service of the prince, and at the will and mandate of the king will transfer themselves to the king and his lordship and will oppose Llywelyn in every way they can.

    (9 November 1277. Treaty of Aberconwy. Edwards, *Littere Wallie*, pp.118–22.)

A.18   With regard to the proposal that the prince should place the lord king in absolute possession of Snowdonia forever and in peace let it be known that since Snowdonia is something which pertains to the principality of Wales, which he and his ancestors have held since the time of *Brutus*, . . . his council does not permit him to renounce that land and take in its place a land in England to which he has less claim. Also the people of Snowdonia say that, even if the prince might wish to convey them to the king's possession, they are unwilling to do *homage* to a stranger with whose language, customs and laws they are unfamiliar. For if that were to happen to them they might be made captive forever and be cruelly treated, as other *cantreds* on every side have been treated by the king's officers and other rulers, more cruel than *Saracens*, as is revealed in the rolls which they sent you holy father.

(November 1282. Llywelyn ap Gruffudd to John Pecham, Archbishop of Canterbury. C.T. Martin, *Registrum Epistolarum fratris Johannis Peckham, Archiepiscopi Cantuariensis*, Rolls Series, II (3 vols.), London, 1882–5, pp.469–71.)

Debating the Evidence

The evidence of the political and diplomatic strategies of the years 1267–83 is, for the most part, contained in a body of letters, charters and treaties, together with the testimony of the Welsh chronicles. The first three groups were among a corpus of public records maintained by the Crown, especially the *Exchequer*, over many centuries. These records are in themselves political. They were kept as a record of the events and motives that impelled government action. The considerations that informed government policy colour the surviving, non-chronicle, evidence. That is not to say that conflicts of opinion do not reverberate through these records. They certainly do. The charters and letters of Llywelyn show the development of his policy just as surely as the contrary strategy of the Crown and the cross-currents among the *Marcher lords* are unfolded.

Source A.1
Does the tone of the Treaty of Montgomery suggest a treaty which offered a 'breathing space' in a protracted conflict or a more lasting settlement? What evidence can be seen in it of Cardinal Ottobuono's mediating role?

Source A.2
The Welsh chronicles at various stages in their composition reflected changed attitudes among the chroniclers themselves to shifts of power in Wales. Is any judgement on the conflict between Llywelyn and his brothers expressed in this record? Why was Llywelyn's victory at Bryn Derwin a serious setback to Henry III's policy in Wales after 1240?

Source A.3

One of the recurrent themes of medieval Welsh history is the way Welsh lords reacted to the direct impact of a strong ruler, be he a Welsh prince or the king of England. What would appear to have been an unsettling factor in Wales in 1256 as far as the magnates were concerned?

Source A.4

Does the document suggest that the act of *fealty*, or paying *homage*, was a purely secular act? What does it imply about the keystone of military control in the Welsh lordships at this time?

Source A.5

Did the Treaty of Montgomery acknowledge the status of Llywelyn as a previously existing right? Does this appear to be consistent with Llywelyn's view of his own status?

Source A.6

Does the letter of Burnell and Merton display a concern to abide by the spirit of the Treaty of Montgomery?

Source A.7

How can this letter demonstrate the importance of Llywelyn's position as Prince of Wales, under the king but receiving the *homage* of other Welsh lords? Does it suggest an alienation between Llywelyn and the Crown at this stage?

Source A.8

Professor Smith cites this document as evidence of Llywelyn's increasing difficulty in retaining the loyalty of stubbornly independent lords who had traditionally owed *fealty* directly to the king. The giving of important hostages to guarantee political acquiescence was a common feature of twelfth- and thirteenth-century politics. Apart from its personal hardship, what might be its impact on dynastic unity?

Source A.9

What phrases in this document betray Llywelyn's growing difficulty in controlling men like *Maredudd ap Rhys Gryg*? Would the terms Llywelyn imposed be likely to endear the Prince of Wales to *Maredudd's* own leading noblemen?

Source A.10

Is it likely that the submission on the part of Gruffudd ap Gwenwynwyn described here was a metaphoric expression used in this record, or an actual ritual act? What would be the importance of an act of submission in the circumstances of this gathering on 17 April 1274?

Source A.11

This document contains the arrangements prescribed to provide for Dafydd ap Gruffydd under the Treaty of Montgomery in 1267. What may be discerned of the 'profile' the King was adopting in these provisions? How might a study of the individuals named as arbitrators in these provisions help to illustrate the network of inter-relations between the Crown and the Welsh lords in the 1260s?

Source A.12

Is there anything in the wording of this document which shows a fundamental difference between the Crown's view of Dafydd's claims in 1277 and its earlier treatment of them in 1267 (Source A.11)?

Source A.13

In view of the fact that Llywelyn's status rested legally on the Treaty of Montgomery, what was the two-edged significance of the demand Llywelyn was making in this document?

Source A.14

The fragments of evidence that we possess concerning the strains and stresses that Llywelyn's policy imposed upon his own subjects show how the jigsaw of historical evidence interlocks:

a) the complaints of Gwynedd representatives in the above document show that Llywelyn was exacting more from his subjects and that it was greatly resented;

b) the substantial sums Llywelyn had to pay to the Crown under the Treaty of Montgomery and for the *homage* of *Maredudd ap Rhys Gryg* are recorded in Public Record Office documents. They have been assessed by Sir Goronwy Edwards as amounting to 13,500 marks between 1267 and about 1274;

c) the military aspects of Llywelyn's ambitious policy, as described by

Professor Smith, imposed enormous costs on Gwynedd in castle-building projects, in the maintenance of a small naval force and repeated recourse to arms.

In Source A.14 itself, what is there about its origin which may incline you to treat the detailed catalogue of woes with some reserve?

Source A.15
Why did Llywelyn feel it was necessary to call the barons of Wales to meet him when Edward I summoned him to pay *homage*? Does this account interpret Llywelyn's refusal to go to the King as a unilateral abrogation of *fealty* by the Prince?

Source A.16
What did Edward I mean by the 'old seed of malice' with reference to Llywelyn's projected marriage with Eleanor de Montfort? Edward might well have viewed the era of *Simon de Montfort* in much the same light as Charles II was later to view the Cromwellian interregnum. How might the recrudescence of a baronial opposition have been of advantage to Llywelyn? Why was Edward especially anxious for the Welsh-born *Dominicans* accompanying Eleanor to be questioned closely?

Source A.17
How was the Treaty of Aberconwy structured so as to enjoin loyalty to the king upon Llywelyn's own subjects even in the event of the Prince's apostasy? Llywelyn had suffered military defeat in 1277, but what other formidable pressure, mentioned in this document, had been brought to bear on him?

Source A.18
Llywelyn's response to Archbishop Pecham's last-minute intervention suggests greater issues at stake than the questions of *feudal* right and responsibility which had hitherto been the ostensible causes of friction. In what way do the points raised here appear to represent an underlying stratum of proto-national or at least ethnic consciousness? Does the document hint at a more direct cause for the astonishingly widespread and immediate support which the Palm Sunday revolt of 1282 received in Wales?

Discussion

With the exception of the excerpts from the Welsh chronicle *Brut y Tywysogyon* (A.2, A.3, A.15) the sources quoted in this section were all originally written in Latin. That pinpoints one of the problems confronting a medieval historian; he is working at one linguistic remove, as it were, from his sources and has to filter his understanding of those sources through his own understanding of the Latin language and its resonances. What is he to make, for example, of the word 'unity' (*unitas* in the Latin) in A.9? What would be the modern equivalent? The historian must also bear in mind that his sources were written by clerics and often have a strong ecclesiastical flavour (A.1, A.2). Does this help us to understand how medieval men viewed the world or does it also conceal the secular motives for their behaviour?

Most of the sources in this section are public documents. In other words, like the statements of politicians today, they take a particular form and are addressed to a public audience. Should we, therefore, take them with a pinch of salt? Thus the Treaty of Montgomery (A.1, A.5) looks like an amicable agreement, but in fact we know that the English only agreed to it reluctantly. A.4 is likewise cast as a 'final concord', that is an agreement between two equal parties, but does its content suggest to you that it was an imposed settlement? Politicians in all ages like grand gestures. The Treaty of Aberconwy (A.17) tells you that Llywelyn agreed to pay a vast indemnity of 50,000 marks. Would it alter your view of the treaty and of Edward I if you knew that this sum was almost immediately pardoned? You will also have noticed that these public documents are full of references to *fealty* and *homage* (A.4, A.5, A.8, A.10, A.15, A.17). The ceremonies of *fealty* and *homage* structure relationships between men in medieval society. Do the frequent references to them in these sources suggest that you should try to understand the ceremonies and their significance before drawing conclusions from the documents?

Three of the sources (A.2, A.3, A.15) are quotations from the Welsh *Chronicle of the Princes* (*Brut y Tywysogyon*). This chronicle was originally written in Latin but soon translated into Welsh. It is from the Welsh translation that these excerpts are taken. Does their style contrast with that of the public documents, such as the treaties? You might notice that the statements they make are almost telegraphic (A.15) and often do not offer an explanation, for example of the quarrel between Llywelyn and his brothers (A.2). But the *Chronicle*, along with Llywelyn's letters (A.7,

A.18), does at least help us to understand the issues from the Welsh as well as from the English angle. It will be clear that Welsh views of Llywelyn were mixed (contrast A.3 and A.14). It is in the thirteenth century, for the first time in the history of Wales, that we can begin to see why men acted as they did and that we can begin to examine the policies of the Welsh princes in their own language. What view of the period would we have if we only had 'English' sources (A.1, A.5, A.6, A.11, A.12, A.16, A.17)? What other types of sources would help to fill out the story? Do you think the medieval historian is permanently handicapped by not having private letters, diaries and tapes, for example?

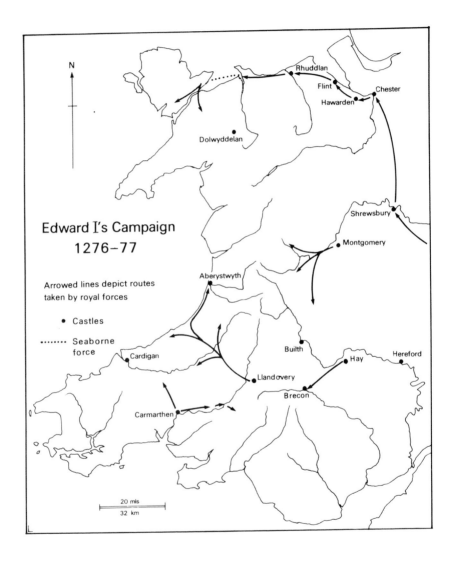

N

Edward I's Campaign
1276-77

Arrowed lines depict routes
taken by royal forces

• Castles

••••••• Seaborne
force

Rhuddlan
Flint
Chester
Hawarden

Dolwyddelan

Shrewsbury

Montgomery

Aberystwyth

Builth

Hereford

Cardigan

Hay

Llandovery

Brecon

Carmarthen

20 mls
32 km

The Edwardian Conquest and its Military Consolidation

IFOR ROWLANDS

The term 'the Edwardian Conquest of Wales' correctly identifies the central role of Edward I but obscures the fact that parts of Wales were under English rule before his accession and that the military subjugation of the remainder involved three campaigns of a different kind and order. Llywelyn ap Gruffudd's refusal, as Edward saw it, to perform *homage* challenged royal overlordship in the most blatant fashion, and in 1276 a punitive expedition was launched to purge the

B.1   contumacy of this disobedient *vassal* (B.1). In the event, Llywelyn's principality was almost destroyed and the balance of power was decisively shifted in the Crown's favour. Confronted in 1282 by a national rebellion against the new disposition in Wales, Edward determined upon the disinheritance of Llywelyn, his dynasty and confederates: a 'just war' against a

B.2   faithless people was to become a war of conquest (B.2). Where the armies of 1277 had halted, those of 1283 pressed on until the already fragile independence of the Welsh was finally extinguished. A third campaign to put down widespread revolts in 1294–5 demonstrated that any attempt to revive it was doomed to failure.

Edward's Welsh wars, like most contemporary campaigns, were wars of manœuvre and attrition in which the aim was not to bring the enemy to battle but to despoil his lands, terrorize his tenantry and methodically reduce his castles. While cavalry composed of household troops and magnate retinues were essential for swift raids, reconnaissance and for the protection of columns of foot on the march, a key role was now assigned to specialists such as garrison troops, crossbowmen and engineers.

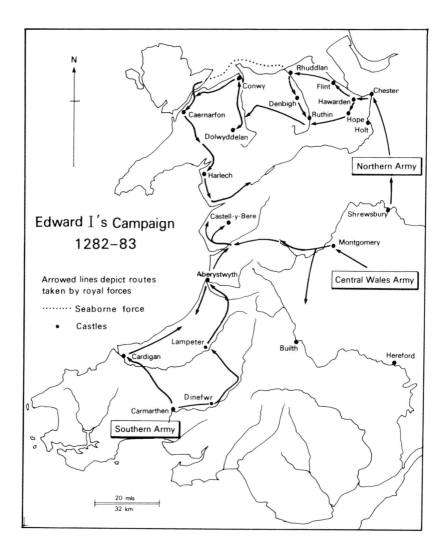

N

Rhuddlan

Conwy

Flint

Chester

Denbigh

Hawarden

Caernarfon

Ruthin

Hope

Holt

Dolwyddelan

Northern Army

Harlech

Castell-y-Bere

Shrewsbury

**Edward I's Campaign
1282–83**

Montgomery

Aberystwyth

Central Wales Army

Arrowed lines depict routes
taken by royal forces

········· Seaborne force

•   Castles

Lampeter

Builth

Hereford

Cardigan

Dinefwr

Carmarthen

Southern Army

20 mils
32 km

Moreover the pace of a campaign was, in large measure, determined by the slow-moving infantry and by the *siege train*, baggage and other impedimenta which often gave an army the appearance of a market town on the move. Above all, a sustained war of movement, in which troops were dispersed for raiding and concentrated for siege, required the establishment and protection of supply lines and *entrepôts*.

Its mountainous terrain, inhospitable climate and heavily wooded approaches made Wales a difficult theatre for large-scale operations. The invader's ability to 'live off the land' was limited and his supply lines might be perilously extended. However, border towns, Marcher castles and royal outposts at Cardigan and Carmarthen — both on tidal waters — could provide bases for initial stockpiling and English naval capability gave them a decisive logistical advantage; Welsh deficiencies in this area were to cost them dear. On land, English armies faced a highly mobile, because lightly armed, infantry whose favoured tactics were ambushes and guerrilla strikes although some native retinues did boast heavy cavalry and siege engines; surprise and speed had to be matched by vigilance and the capacity to concentrate troops swiftly at the point of need. Welsh castles of stone were few in number and, although some incorporated in a modest way the latest advances in design, they generally presented few problems to English siege armies — in no field were the discrepancies in resources so manifest. Once the Crown had decided to put a large army into the field, its vastly superior resources in manpower, money and materials and its efficient commissariat should ensure victory unless, as had happened in the past, its advance ground to a halt through inadequate provisioning, physical exhaustion or a commander's military timidity.

The war proclaimed in November 1276 did not really gather momentum until the following spring but early gains were made in the critical area of the Middle March by lords such as *Humphrey de Bohun* and Ralph de Tosney who now enjoyed royal support in the recovery of lost territory. The more elaborate and more laboriously assembled royal offensive involved the co-ordinated advance of three armies from commands at Chester, Montgomery and Carmarthen. The central and southern armies were to contain Llywelyn within Snowdonia by securing the upper Severn and subduing his allies in Deheubarth. They encountered but little opposition as, one by one, the Welsh castles capitulated — Dolforwyn, after a week's siege, in April 1277. By early June, the fortresses of the Tywi valley had fallen into English hands and the occupation of Llanbadarn on 25 July marked the end of Welsh resistance in Deheubarth. Llywelyn's southern *homagers* with almost indecent haste sought the 'king's peace' and, as they did so, his principality began to disintegrate

B.3 (B.3). Even so the northern army, charged with a frontal assault upon the lordship of Snowdon itself, proceeded with great caution. The area of the middle Dee and northern Powys was cleared of hostile elements before Edward's arrival at Chester on 15 July. Thence, his advance to the mouth of the Conwy hinged on the new castle-bases he built at Flint and Rhuddlan — both capable of being supplied by sea. Assured of supplies and fall-back positions, he struck out in late August at the soft underbelly of Llywelyn's defences by sending an amphibious force to the island granary of Anglesey. This landing on his northern flank, the loss of essential summer crops and the

B.4 defection of his allies persuaded Llywelyn to capitulate (B.4).

If this nine-month war had cruelly exposed the military ineffectiveness and political irresolution of Llywelyn and his allies, it had with equal clarity revealed the formidable strengths of his opponent. Edward's firm resolve and vastly greater resources were channelled into the war effort by a household administration that proved to be an admirably flexible instrument for both financial supervision and military co-ordination. Access to Italian credit provided ready cash to pay for the men and war materials culled from England, France, Wales and Ireland. Hundreds of axemen had been deployed in the essential task of clearing wide passes through wooded country but even these numbers were dwarfed by the infantry contingents that Edward had assembled — at one stage, as many as 15,000 foot were on his payroll. Chiefly bowmen, these had been recruited from the border counties, from Welsh communities within the March or demanded of Welsh loyalists. Problems of pay and supply and a high rate of desertion reduced their number and effectiveness but their sheer mass must have shaken enemy morale. At sea, Edward's flotilla had not only disembarked a major force on the Anglesey beaches but would have played a key role in enforcing his embargo upon the movement of goods into Wales (B.5). Finally, the active support of Llywelyn's Welsh enemies — the lord of southern Powys and *Dafydd ap Gruffudd* not the least amongst them — proved doubly valuable: militarily, because Edward could concentrate his resources for an assault upon Snowdonia and, politically, because he could be seen as an enforcer of rights denied by Llywelyn to his own *vassals* (B.6).

    Losing face but keeping his title, Llywelyn was henceforth to be confined to Snowdonia and Anglesey, his truncated principality encircled by vastly enlarged Crown lands (especially so in Deheubarth) and by pliant native lordships. This confinement was as much military as political — Llywelyn's isolation was secured by an extensive castle-building programme in the occupied territories. Royal money was committed to the repair of former Welsh fortresses such as Carreg Cennen, Dinefwr and Dinas Brân and such lordship castles as Hawarden, but the greatest sum was lavished upon the construction of formidable stone castles on new sites at Flint, Rhuddlan and Aberystwyth and on the addition of masonry defences to the existing site at Builth. These four incorporated all that was best in contemporary military architecture: high and immensely thick *curtain walling* used in combination with projecting mural towers. Fighting platforms at wall-top level and arrow loops set in curtain and tower enabled the garrison to bring a heavy concentration of firepower to bear both from above and across the flanks. Tower and curtain could thus be used to cover an entire site by integrating two or more enclosures or wards longitudinally or side by side, thus presenting a series of obstacles to the enemy; when an inner and more formidably defended circuit was enclosed by an outer ring of defences, the resulting *concentric* plan made these obstacles virtually insurmountable. The entrance was protected by placing it between two exceptionally strong projecting towers and great ingenuity was devoted to the defence of the massive *gatehouses* thus created.

    Edward's own involvement in the construction of his new

B.7

B.8

B.9

B.10

Welsh castles was constant and detailed but an equally important contribution was made by his Savoyard architects and masons, most notably Master James of St George, whose influence can be detected in overall design, architectural detail and building technique (B.7). Wherever possible, these castles were built on coastal sites and, at Rhuddlan, the River Clwyd was diverted to link the castle to the sea. Work at the four sites was set in motion in the summer of 1277 and carried on with such speed that it was almost complete by 1282. This achievement was a triumph of organization, as huge quantities of materials had to be transported by land and sea for distribution to the building sites and a large labour force — as many as 3,000 men at one stage — had to be recruited, supplied and paid. The £30,000 expended on these works exceeded the cost of the war itself and was a measure of the King's commitment to the new order in Wales.

Yet this new order was deeply flawed. Partial conquest and containment had created a potentially explosive mixture. Those Welsh lords who had escaped disinheritance were increasingly frustrated by their political subordination; unconquered, they asserted their rights only to find them challenged or circumscribed by the Crown. Welsh communities in the occupied territories increasingly resented the high-handedness of royal officials and their insensitive disregard for native law and custom (B.8). Llywelyn, who must have felt the humiliation more keenly than most, held his hand but could clearly see that Welsh independence would in time be nullified by unqualified acceptance of Edward's interpretation of his overlordship. Central to that concept was jurisdictional control which meant in essence that even Prince Llywelyn might be peremptorily summoned like any less exalted (B.9). His dignity was not easily assuaged by the King's exaggerated punctiliousness, rather was it the more affronted — as in the Arwystli dispute — by the latter's ill-concealed partisanship. Tension between Welsh and English crystallized into a conflict of laws in which law was seen as a badge of national identity (B.10). Llywelyn, who had the most to lose, was reluctant to turn it into a conflict of arms: others were not and in the spring of 1282 an assault by his brother Dafydd upon Hawarden triggered off a series of revolts throughout much of Wales. Llywelyn's unique claim to Welsh leadership ensured his participation — a national rebellion thus became 'Llywelyn's war'.

B.11   A number of castles, including Aberystwyth, were taken but early gains were not pressed home and the element of surprise was soon dissipated. With his key fortresses still holding out, Edward began to mobilize all available resources (B.11). Military commands were soon established at Chester, Montgomery and Carmarthen and, from the latter, two armies were assembled for the task of retaking the castles of mid and south-west Wales and mopping up pockets of Welsh resistance before converging upon Snowdonia to support the major thrust by the third army along the northern littoral. Here, Edward's advance was cautious, methodical and relentless. The reduction of the Four Cantreds (accomplished by mid-October) would enable his army to link up with the force sent to Anglesey and engaged, since late August, in building a bridge of boats across the Menai

B.12 (B.12). The King's advance was, however, halted by two unwelcome initiatives — the one diplomatic, the other military. Archbishop Pecham's autumn negotiations with the Welsh were doubtless inspired by Christian charity but they were not productive. The Welsh presented him with a catalogue of grievances which listed the abuses perpetrated by English officials and, above all, insisted on their vulnerability when

B.13 unprotected by their own native laws and customs (B.13). Edward, on his part, made it clear that the price of peace was the extinction of Llywelyn's principality and the disinheritance of

B.14 his dynasty (B.14). In the mean time, and without the King's permission, the English force in Anglesey attempted a crossing of the Menai Straits but it was repulsed with heavy losses. Edward, his mind now set on a winter campaign, patiently built up his forces; Llywelyn, in an attempt to disperse this concentration of enemy troops closing in on Snowdonia, struck southwards towards Builth. This break-out, though strategically sound, proved disastrous, for on 11 December 1282, he was killed in an engagement with a Marcher contingent within a

B.15 mile or so of Edward's new castle there (B.15).

    To the bards his death, like a calamity of nature, was of

B.16 almost cosmic significance (B.16). In military terms it settled the outcome of the war. In the month that followed, the Conwy was crossed, Dolwyddelan was taken and English forces were transported across the Menai making possible an advance via Caernarfon to Harlech. By 14 January the southern army had retaken Aberystywyth, having in the previous summer cleared the Tywi valley of insurgents. The last vestige of organized resistance was snuffed out in April when the central army took Castell y Bere from which *Dafydd ap Gruffudd* had sought to continue the unavailing struggle. Two months later this unconvincing patriot was delivered up to the English by his own countrymen (B.17). In July Edward disbanded his field army — the task of conquest had, it seemed, been accomplished.

B.17

The second war, like the first, had been won not by brilliant feats of generalship or decisive battles but by the efficient garnering and intelligent deployment of resources. Welsh resistance was ground down by the patient amassing of men and material: in one sense, Welsh independence did not as much perish in a clash of arms as suffocate in a welter of parchment. The humdrum, unspectacular but vitally essential work was done as much by Edward's administrators as by his soldiers. Once more provisions were purveyed from the Crown's wide dominions and transported to the points of distribution (B.18). Once more household troops and magnate retinues were afforced by large numbers of infantry with as many as 3–4,000 attached to each army (B.19). Everything in 1282–3 was done on a larger scale: as many as 1,500 Gascon crossbowmen were on the king's payroll and his fleet had increased to forty vessels more. With the armies having been kept in the field for a much longer time, the total cost of some £150,000 dwarfed that incurred in 1276–7 — it was the price Edward was prepared to pay to put an end to 'the malice of the Welsh'.

B.18

B.19

This chivalric triumph was celebrated by an 'Arthurian' tournament at Nefyn and Welsh defeat by the transference to Westminster of the *Croes Naid* and Llywelyn's coronet. Hostages were taken from the vanquished and the suspect, and very few of the princely dynasties survived the débâcle. The conquest was to be further consolidated by a castle-building programme even more extensive than that inaugurated in 1277 and one which had been planned as early as the spring of 1282 (B.20).

B.20

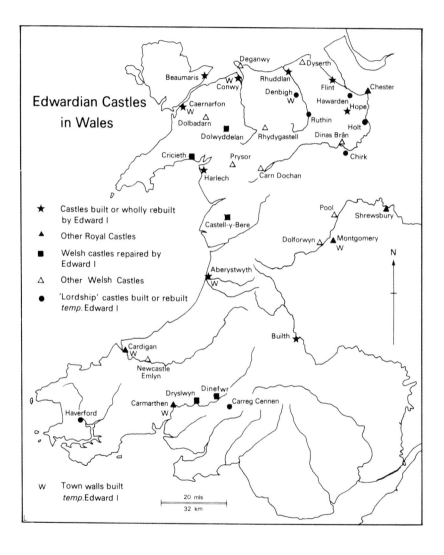

Edwardian Castles in Wales

★ Castles built or wholly rebuilt by Edward I

▲ Other Royal Castles

■ Welsh castles repaired by Edward I

△ Other Welsh Castles

● 'Lordship' castles built or rebuilt *temp.* Edward I

W Town walls built *temp.* Edward I

20 mls
32 km

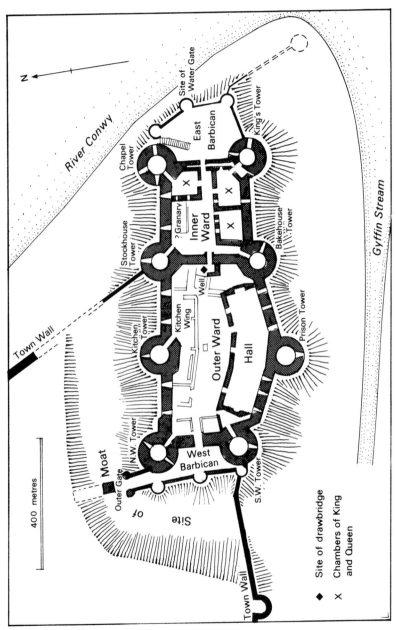

Plan of Conwy Castle.

Site of drawbridge ♦

Chambers of King and Queen ✕

River Conwy

Gyffin Stream

Site of Water Gate

East Barbican

King's Tower

Chapel Tower

Stockhouse Tower

?Granary

Inner Ward

Bakehouse Tower

Well

Prison Tower

Kitchen Tower

Kitchen Wing

Outer Ward

Hall

Town Wall

Moat

N.W. Tower

Outer Gate

West Barbican

S.W. Tower

Site of

Town Wall

400 metres

N

50

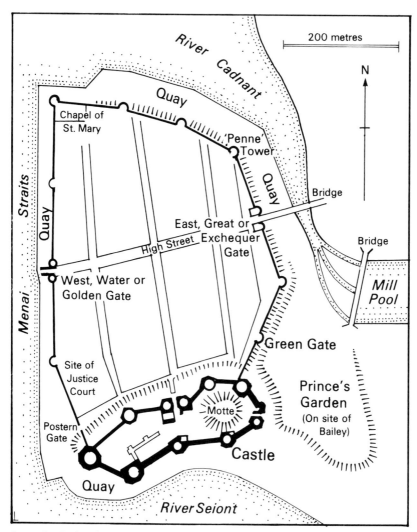

Caernarfon Castle and town.

Any future rebellion was to be contained by an inner circle of castles which would suck in the enemy's assaults until a large army could be put into the field. Welsh castles such as Cricieth and Castell y Bere were repaired and new Marcher strongholds were built at Denbigh and Holt, but the greatest commitment was to the construction of massive royal castles at Conwy (begun in March 1283) and at Harlech and Caernarfon (begun in June 1283). Summonses were sent to almost every county in England for woodcutters, carpenters, masons and diggers until as many as 4,000 men laboured at the three sites in 1283–4 (B.21). Material and money were transported from England, France and Ireland in huge quantities — indeed, the latter dominion paid for more than half the building costs over the next five years. Urged on by the King, the works were carried on with such urgency that Conwy was virtually completed by late 1287, Harlech by 1289 and at Caernarfon — the grandest of all — two-thirds of the work had been accomplished by 1292. All these castles exhibited the skill of James of St George, now Master of the King's Works in Wales, in the application of architectural technique to a chosen site. All were characterized by solidity of construction, immense thickness of wall and tower and great sophistication of defences. At Caernarfon — the Roman Segontium — traditional associations with the imperial past were given architectural expression by its banded walls and polygonal towers modelled on those of Rome's successor state at Constantinople. Its high turrets and the stone eagles that once crowned its largest tower made Caernarfon the secular cathedral of the conquest. The symbolism was two-edged — the Eagles' Lair (*Eryri* in Welsh) was now in English hands.

B.21

By 1301 some £80,000 had been spent on the King's works in Wales. This huge sum not only included the cost of a new castle at Beaumaris (begun after the Welsh revolt of 1294–5) but also defences for the plantation boroughs which Edward founded in 1277 (Flint, Rhuddlan and Aberystwyth) and in 1282–3 (Conwy, Caernarfon and Harlech). Physically attached to their castles and exclusively the preserve of privileged and non-native settlers, these fortified towns had their part to play in the military consolidation of the conquest. The *burgesses*, subject to

the jurisdiction of the castle constable, were responsible for the
B.22   town's defence (B.22). They formed essential support units to
B.23   the substantial garrisons now established (B.23). The *bastide*
character of these new towns was most evident in their defences
and especially so when these — as at Conwy and Caernarfon —
were comprised of stout walls, mural towers and *gatehouses*.
These garrisons and *burgesses* (not a few of whom were war
veterans) formed the cutting-edge of a new wave of colonial
settlement.

Their vigilance and preparedness was soon tested. In 1277–8
a revolt by *Rhys ap Maredudd* — a disaffected collaborator of the
wars — was swiftly crushed but not before an army of over
25,000 men had been mobilized. More serious, because more
widespread, was the rising which broke out in 1294–5 as a
violent backlash against military occupation, fiscal exploitation
and oppressive officialdom. Under-strength garrisons were
besieged, others were isolated and Caernarfon itself was taken.
The colonial regime wobbled under the impact but, as the key
fortresses held out, Edward had time to assemble a huge army
which included at one stage more than 35,000 foot. The lost
castles were retaken and the others relieved and by March 1295
Welsh stamina had been exhausted. Edward's castle-building
programme had proved its worth. So much so that it was now
extended to include a new castle at Beaumaris in Anglesey. The
urgency with which the work there was undertaken reflected
continuing official concern about the volatility of affairs in
B.24   Wales (B.24).

Even so Edward's last demonstration of military might on
Welsh soil had proved sufficient. Three campaigns within
twenty years had deprived the Welsh of their natural leaders,
drained them of resources and destroyed their capacity for
resistance. An economically under-resourced, militarily back-
ward and politically divided people — ever a volatile element
within the *Plantaganet* dominions — had been ground to
submission by an infinitely more powerful neighbour. The
conquest did bring peace, or rather what might pass for peace in
a still-troubled and divided land, but it was a peace which lasted
for more than a century though periodically punctuated by
outbreaks of disorder such as occurred in the 1340s. Then,

Caernarfon Castle. (*Source: Cadw: Welsh Historic Monuments. Crown Copyright.*)

The Theodosian Wall of Constantinople. *(Source Cadw: Welsh Historic Monuments. Crown Copyright.)*

B.25 nervous English colonists looked back with nostalgia to the days of 'Edward the Conqueror' and to 'the Conquest' which was that monarch's greatest military achievement (B.25). The durability of that achievement was however to depend in large measure upon the civilian governance that the same victorious king imposed upon the vanquished people.

Sources

B.1 . . . It is agreed by the common counsel of all the aforesaid prelates, barons and others that the king shall not hear the aforesaid petition of Llywelyn, and shall not admit his excuses . . . but that he shall go against Llywelyn as his rebel and disturber of his peace and that all those who hold of the king in chief and owe him service shall be summoned to be at Worcester at Midsummer next with horses and arms . . . to set out with the king into Wales against Llywelyn . . .

(17 November 1276. Decision of a Great Council held at Westminster. *Calendar of Close Rolls 1272–9*, pp.360–1.)

B.2 . . . the king proposes . . . to put an end finally to the matter he has now commenced of putting down the malice of the Welsh, as Llywelyn ap Gruffudd and other Welshmen, his accomplices, have so many times disturbed the peace of the realm in the king's time and the time of his progenitors and they persist in their resumed rebellion and the king conceives it to be more convenient and suitable that he and the inhabitants of his realm should be burdened on this occasion with labours and expenses in order to put down wholly their malice for the common good . . .

(24 November 1282. A letter sent to the sheriffs of England. *Calendar of Welsh Rolls*, pp. 275–6.)

B.3 . . . And then *Rhys ap Maredudd* ap Rhys and Rhys Wyndod, nephew of the prince, made a pact with Pain de Chaworth. And Llywelyn, brother of Rhys Wyndod, and Hywel ap Rhys Gryg left their land and went to Llywelyn. And Rhys (Fychan ap Rhys) ap Maelgwn went to *Roger de Mortimer*, his kinsman, and promised in his hand submission to the king. And last of all Deheubarth, there submitted to the English the two sons of Maredudd ab Owain, Gruffudd and Cynan, and Llywelyn ab Owain, their nephew. And then Pain, and with him a mighty host, came to subjugate three *commotes* above the Aeron — Nanhuniog and Mefenydd and *Cwmwd* Perfedd.

(1277. T. Jones (ed.), *Brut y Tywysogyon or the Chronicle of the Princes, Peniarth MS 20 Version*, Cardiff, 1952, p.118.)

B.4   And about the beginning of autumn the king sent many of his host in ships to burn Anglesey and to carry off much of its corn. After that the prince came, about the Calends of Winter, to Rhuddlan to the king and made peace with him. And the king invited him to London at Christmas; and he went at the invitation. And in London he tendered his *homage* to the king on Christmas day. And after staying there a fortnight he returned again.

(1277. Jones, *Brut y Tywysogyon, Peniarth MS 20 Version*, p.119.)

B.5   And the king from now inhibits . . . that throughout England, Ireland and Gascony it shall be inhibited that from henceforth no one shall communicate with Llywelyn or his aiders . . . and that no one shall take into their land, or permit to be taken thither through their land or power, by land or by sea, victuals, horses, arms or other things that may be useful to men in any way.

(17 November 1276. Decision taken at a Great Council held at Westminster. *Calendar of Close Rolls 1272–9*, p.361.)

B.6   *Dafydd ap Gruffudd* demanded of the messenger, and still continues to demand, that payment of wages be made to his two horsemen and all his footmen, as to other knights and footmen. And the Earl of Warwick, who was greatly disturbed on this account, fearing lest Dafydd might withdraw from the king's service with his men unless he was satisfied, ordered the writer to pay the men of the aforesaid Dafydd . . .

(About 4 April 1277. Letter of Ralph de Basages, a royal clerk, to Edward I. Edwards, *Calendar of Ancient Correspondence concerning Wales*, p.67.)

B.7   8 April. To Master James *Ingeniator* in payment of his wages for
       17 days up to the present . . . . 17*s.*
       To the same James going into Wales to oversee the
       works of the castles there, for his wages and expenses
       from now until Sunday next after St John *ante Portam
       Latinam* for
       29 days . . . . 58*s.*
   20 May. To the same for his wages for 3 months following when
       he was out of court visiting the castles of Flint and
       Rhuddlan . . . . £8. 8*s.*

(1278. Extracts from a royal household (Wardrobe) account. A. J. Taylor, 'Master James of St George', *English Historical Review*, LXV (1950), pp. 433–4.)

B.8   Because of these grievances and the other things which the said
       Reginald did to us and his threats to behead any envoys we
       might send to the court of the lord king to seek justice, because
       we have endured many other losses and suffered many injuries
       — when we used to send envoys to the lord king's court they
       were not permitted, and did not dare, to enter — we have, on
       account of these complaints, deemed ourselves free from the
       oath we took before God to the lord king.

(November 1282. Grievances of the men of Rhos against Reginald de Grey, Justiciar of Chester. C. T. Martin, *Registrum Epistolarum fratris Johannis Peckham, Archiepiscopi Cantuariensis*, II, p.451.)

B.9   The king does not understand and is unable to understand the
       article of the peace concluded between him and Llywelyn of
       which Llywelyn's letters make mention, to wit concerning the
       hearing and determining of pleas and controversies in the
       Marches of Wales and in Wales, in any other way than it was
       always usual and accustomed in the times of his predecessors
       and in his own time, nor can it be elicited from the wording of

the peace otherwise than that controversies and contentions in the Marches ought to be heard and determined according to the laws of the Marches and those arising in Wales ought to be heard and determined according to the Welsh laws at certain days and places that he shall cause to be prefixed to the parties. Therefore Llywelyn shall come before the king's justices in those parts at days and places that they shall make known to him to do and receive what justice shall dictate according to the laws aforesaid . . .

(14 July 1279. Letter of Edward I to Llywelyn ap Gruffudd. *Calendar of Welsh Rolls*, p.175.)

B.10   And the aforesaid Prince Llywelyn declared that the fact that each province under the lord king's dominion — the Gascons in Gascony, the Scots in Scotland, the Irish in Ireland and the English in England — has its own laws and customs, according to the mode and usage of those parts in which they are situate, amplified rather than diminished the Crown. In the same wise he seeks to have his own Welsh law and to be able to proceed by it, especially as the lord king had of his own free will in the peace made between them, granted their own law to him and to all Welshmen. As a matter of common right the Welsh, like these other nations subject to the king's governance, ought to have their own laws and customs according to their race (Latin: *linguam*).

(1279. J. Conway Davies, *The Welsh Assize Roll, 1277–84*, p.266.)

B.11   Begs to be excused from sending her the aid which he promised for her war in Provence because he needs all his resources for the war which Llywelyn and his brother Dafydd are waging against him in Wales. Roger de Clifford has been taken prisoner, many of his men have been slain, and one of the king's castles in that region is occupied; wherefore the whole army is needed to put down that rebellion.

(8 April 1282. Letter of Edward I to Queen Margaret of France. Edwards, *Calendar of Ancient Correspondence*, p.56.)

B.12   To all the king's barons and subjects of the Cinque Ports in his garrison in Anglesey. Writ of aid in favour of Luke de Tany whom the king is sending in garrison and defence of those parts and to provide and make a bridge there and order to cause him to have cords and anchors necessary for the construction of the bridge as he shall direct.

(18 August 1282. *Calendar of Welsh Rolls*, p.235.)

B.13   They assert that just as all Christians have their laws and customs in their own lands — even as the Jews in England have their laws — they themselves and their predecessors had, in their own territories, their own and immutable laws and customs until the English took their laws away from them after the last war.

(November 1282. Complaints of the sons of Maredudd ab Owain to John Pecham. Martin, *Registrum Epistolarum*, II, p.454.)

B.14   These are to be conveyed to the king in secret: firstly, the king's barons believe his will to be this, namely, that if the lord Llywelyn were to submit himself to the king's grace, the king would honourably provide him with land worth £1,000 sterling . . . in any place in England but only if the aforesaid Llywelyn were to place the lord king in absolute, free and perpetual possession of Snowdonia.

(November 1282. Part of the terms proposed to Llywelyn ap Gruffudd. Martin, *Registrum Epistolarum*, II, p.467.)

B.15   Sire,
Know that the stout men whom you assigned to my command fought against Llywelyn ap Gruffudd in the region of Builth on the Friday next after the feast of St Nicholas and that Llywelyn ap Gruffudd is dead, his army vanquished and the whole flower of his army killed, as the bearer of this letter will tell you and have credence in what he will tell you on my part.

(Immediately after 11 December 1282. J. E. Morris, 'Two Documents relating to the Conquest of Wales', *English Historical Review*, XIV, p.507.)

B.16   Poni welwch-chwi'r haul yn hwylaw-'r awyr?
Poni welwch-chwi'r sŷr wedi 'r syrthiaw?
Poni chredwch-chwi i Dduw, ddyniadon ynfyd?
Poni welwch-chwi'r byd wedi 'r bydiaw?
Och hyd atat-ti, Dduw, na ddaw — mor dros dir!

(See you not the sun hurtling the sky?
See you not that the stars have fallen?
Have you no belief in God, foolish men?
See you not that the world's ending?
Ah God, that the sea would cover the land!)

(Gruffudd ap yr Ynad Coch's lament upon the death of Llywelyn ap Gruffudd. T. Parry, *The Oxford Book of Welsh Verse*, pp.47–8 and G. Jones, *The Oxford Book of Welsh Verse in English*, pp.32–3.)

B.17   The tongue of man can scarcely recount the evil deeds committed by the Welsh upon the king's progenitors and him by invasions of the realm from time within memory . . . but God, wishing, as it seems, to put an end to these evil proceedings has, after the prince had been slain, destined David, as the last survivor of the family of traitors aforesaid, to the king's prison after he had been captured by men of his own race.

(28 June 1283. Letter of Edward I to the earls and barons of England. *Calendar of Welsh Rolls*, p.281.)

B.18   William Bagot is appointed to provide the king in the counties of Gloucester, Salop and Stafford with corn for the king's armies of Wales and to ordain that all corn that can be bought in those counties in any fairs and markets shall be carried to Shrewsbury, Montgomery and Oswestry for the munition of the said armies coming thither.

(2 June 1282. General notification to the king's officials and subjects. *Calendar of Welsh Rolls*, p.224.)

B.19   Writ of aid in favour of Richard de Bosco, his knight, whom the king is sending to those parts to make provision of 2,500

	Wood Cutters	Diggers		Carpenters		Masons		Totals		
		a	b	a	b	a	b	a	b	All
Bucks/Beds		50	0	20	0	0	0	70	0	70
Cambs/Hunts		50	0	20	0	0	0	70	0	70
Cheshire		0	100	0	0	0	0	0	100	100
Cumberland		10	0	10	0	0	0	20	0	20
Derby/Notts	•	20	0	10	0	0	30	30	30	60
Essex/Herts		50	0	20	0	0	0	70	0	70
Gloucester	•	0	0	0	25	15	0	15	25	40
Hampshire		40	0	10	0	0	0	50	0	50
Hereford	•	0	0	0	0	0	0	0	0	0
Kent		20	0	15	0	0	0	35	0	35
Lincolnshire		150	0	40	0	0	20	190	20	210
Norfolk/Suffolk		100	0	20	0	0	0	120	0	120
Northants		100	0	20	0	0	0	120	0	120
Northumberland		40	0	10	0	0	0	50	0	50
Oxford/Berks		30	0	20	0	0	0	50	0	50
Rutland		10	0	10	10	0	20	20	30	50
Salop/Staffs	•	40	0	15	40	0	30	55	70	125
Somerset/Dorset		0	0	0	0	15	0	0	15	15
Surrey/Sussex		50	0	20	0	0	0	70	0	70
Warwick/Leics	•	50	0	15	0	0	0	65	0	65
Wiltshire	•	20	0	10	0	0	0	30	0	30
Worcestershire		20	0	20	0	0	0	40	0	40
Yorkshire		150	0	40	0	0	20	190	20	210
Totals		1000	100	345	75	30	120	1360	310	1670

*woodcutters supplied (numbers not specified) by county but 1600 in total

a workers impressed in 1282

b workers impressed in 1283

Fifteen masons from Somerset and fifteen from Gloucestershire gathered at Bristol to build Aberystwyth castle. All other workers gathered at Chester to construct the North Wales castles and the castle at Builth.

The impressment of men for the King's works in Wales, 1282–3.

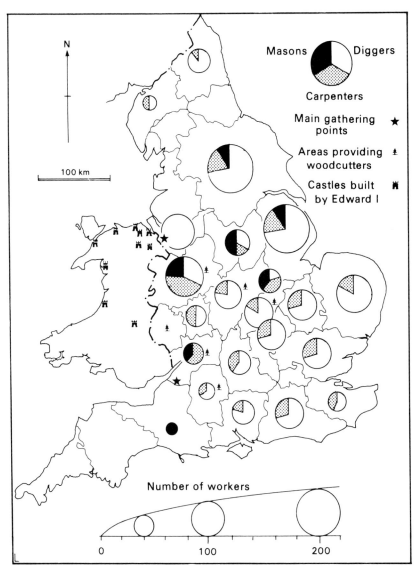

The impressment of men for the King's works in north Wales 1282–3.
(see table opposite).

footmen by election and to conduct them to the king at Montgomery, so that they shall be there in the *quinzaine* of Easter next at the latest, ready to set out in person with the king for the parts of Meirionnydd against the Welsh rebels.

(21 March 1283. Letter to the sheriff of Salop and Stafford. *Calendar of Welsh Rolls*, p.280.)

B.20   N.B. to seek 300 (500) carpenters from the counties to be sent to Chester so that they are there by a fortnight after Whitsun. Urgent.

Also the maximum number of 1,000–2,000 diggers to be at Chester by the same date. Carpenters and diggers are to be distrained by constables. One captain constable to be over the carpenters. Control of the diggers to be left to your discretion, provided that whoever is sent to seek them is their chief leader and other constables are appointed under him. Urgent.

Also N.B. to ask for salt meat from Gascony.

(About mid-April 1282. Minutes of a meeting of royal officials. A. J. Taylor, 'Castlebuilding in Wales in the later thirteenth century: the prelude to construction', E.M. Jope (ed.), *Studies in Building History*, p.112.)

B.21   Order to cause provision to be made of 40 carpenters and 150 diggers in his *bailiwick* and to cause them to be conducted to the king at Chester by one of the *sheriff's* men, so that they shall be there in the octaves of Holy Trinity next, to do the king's order and that the person so conducting may be answerable to the king for their bodies there, as the king needs carpenters and diggers for his works in Wales. The *sheriff* shall cause them to have their wages from the day when they commence their journey until they arrive at Chester when the king shall cause them to have their wages.

(15 April 1282. Letter to the Sheriff of York. *Calendar of Welsh Rolls*, pp.247–8.)

B.22   That is to say that each of the *burgesses* ... or the heirs and assigns of each of them being Englishmen, shall find an armed man in the aforesaid town of Denbigh for the guard and defence of the aforesaid town of Denbigh for each *burgage* and *curtilage* beforenamed . . . And if any of the aforesaid *burgesses* . . . shall fail to guard or defend the said town of Denbigh by himself or an armed man . . . it shall be lawful for us or our heirs . . . to seize and retain in our hands . . . each *burgage* and *curtilage* in respect of which the above-mentioned service was not performed.

(Between 1295 and 1305. Charter of Henry de Lacy for Denbigh. A. Ballard and J. Tait, *British Borough Charters, 1212–1307*, pp.114–15.)

B.23 The king has committed to John de Havering during pleasure his castle of Caernarfon, with the armour and all things forming the munition of the castle, and has granted him 200 marks yearly for the custody, to be received by the hands of the Chamberlain, on condition that he shall have continuously in garrison there, in addition to himself and his household and at his cost, 40 fencible men of whom 15 shall be crossbowmen, one artiller, a carpenter, a mason and a smith, and of the others shall be made janitors, watchmen and other necessary ministers in the castle.

(21 October 1284. *Calendar of Welsh Rolls*, p.291.)

B.24 Sirs,
   As our lord the king has commanded us, by letters of the *Exchequer*, to let you have a clear picture of all aspects of the state of the works at Beaumaris, so that you may be able to lay down the level of work for this coming season . . . we write to inform you that the work . . . is very costly and we need a great deal of money . . . As to how things are in the land of Wales, we still cannot be any too sure. But, as you well know, Welshmen are Welshmen, and you need to understand them properly; if, which God forbid, there is war with France and Scotland, we shall need to watch them all the more closely.

(27 February 1296. Report of Master James of St George and Walter of Winchester. J. G. Edwards, 'Edward I's Castle-building in Wales', *Proceedings of the British Academy*, XXXII

(1946), pp.80–1 and translated in A. J. Taylor, *The King's Works in Wales 1277–1330*, pp.398–9.)

B.25   They desire to inform the prince that his Englishmen residing in boroughs ... were never since the conquest in such perilous plight as they are now. The prince's grandfather, Edward the conqueror of Wales, established towns and castles there, caused them to be inhabited by Englishmen, and gave them various *franchises* by his charter.

(Shortly after 14 February 1345. Letter from the community of Rhuddlan to Edward, Prince of Wales. Edwards, *Calendar of Ancient Correspondence*, pp.231–2.)

Debating the Evidence

It is a truism that war is the forcing-ground of innovation in many fields. This can be said of science and technology and, in medieval times, of architecture and engineering too. Edward I's wars in Wales appear to have forced another kind of growth — documentary records. The wars of 1277 and 1282–3 presented massive logistical problems and the efforts required to overcome them demanded enormous expense and a frenetic pace of work. The heightened level of government activity and the great financial responsibilities undertaken by the Crown and its officials made effective record-keeping vital. The body of official records, preserved largely in parchment rolls, which record royal decisions and account for government expenditure must be seen in the light of Edward I's awareness, recorded in Document B.2, that the 1282 campaign was to be a once-and-for-all effort to settle the 'Welsh question'.

Source B.1
What evidence does this document offer about *feudal* military organization? Is this response to the challenge posed by Llywelyn in 1276 represented as the personal reaction of his *feudal* overlord?

Source B.2
Is there any element of 'case-making' in this letter to the *sheriffs* of the shires? Why would their role be vital in any campaign? How does the

King justify the large-scale expenditure being undertaken for the 1282 campaign in Wales? What might have prompted the King to issue such a letter to his *sheriffs* — his main channel of communication with the shires?

Source B.3

Ifor Rowlands has referred to the 'indecent haste' with which the west Wales lords made their accommodations with the Crown in 1277. Which of the following factors would you rate most highly as contributing to the collapse:
a) dynastic rivalries between the descendants of the Lord Rhys;
b) the proximity of west Wales to powerful Marcher lordships;
c) resentment and suspicion of Gwynedd's pre-eminence?
Why would the affairs of Deheubarth be likely to loom large in the chronicle *Brut y Tywysogyon*? As a monastic chronicle associated with St Davids and Cistercian houses at Whitland, Strata Florida and Cwm-hir, what kind of distinctive features might be expected of it?

Source B.4

How might an autumn raid on the isle of Anglesey be likely to have a dramatic effect on Gwynedd? Does this extract suggest or assume cause and effect in this instance?

Source B.5

What modern terminology might be appropriate to describe the King's strategy as outlined in this record?

Source B.6

Does the author of the article attribute the concern for *Dafydd ap Gruffudd's* position reflected in this document to:
a) Dafydd's importance as a military asset;
b) Dafydd's personal political support in Wales;
c) Dafydd's value as a symbol of Llywelyn's breach of *feudal* obligations?

Source B.7

Is there anything in this record which appears to attach either a higher importance or a greater difficulty to Master James's work in Wales than to his previous duties? How else might the relationship between Savoyard military architecture and the Edwardian castles in Wales have come to light if no records had survived concerning Master James and his work?

Source B.8
What crucial part of the *feudal* relationship between *vassal* and Crown did the men of Rhos consider to have been abrogated by Reginald de Grey's activities?

Sources B.9 and B.10
How might Llywelyn's claim that the persistence of differing national laws and customs within the king's realms 'amplified rather than diminished the Crown' be explained? Of what much later political concept is this pluralistic view redolent, bearing in mind the fact that the terms used by Llywelyn were *'nationes'* for provinces and *'imperium'* for dominion?

Source B.9
How far does Edward I's statement in this letter give a clear definition of the jurisdiction to be observed in disputes between a Welsh lord and a *Marcher lord*?

Source B.11
This letter is cited as evidence of Edward's efforts to muster his forces for action. What broader conclusion might also be drawn from it about the impact of the 1282 war?

Source B.12
What conclusion can be drawn from this document about Edward I's proposed strategy?

Source B.13
What, other than a legalistic argument about jurisdiction of laws, might be discerned in this statement?

Source B.14
How might Edward I's objectives as *feudal* overlord be fulfilled by the proposal outlined here? On what grounds, other than personal devotion to Gwynedd, was Llywelyn's response to such a proposal likely to be negative?

Source B.15
What is the relative importance of this terse document compared with the more detailed accounts to be found in several other chronicles?

Source B.16
Gruffudd ab yr Ynad Coch (son of the Red Justice), in addition to being a court bard, was probably a member of the *curial* or official class that had developed in the fledgeling principality of Gwynedd since about 1200.

Source B.17
What is there about this document, different though it is from the bard's lament above, which in any way parallels it?

Sources B.18, B.19, B.20, B.21
What light does this series of documents throw upon the demands of successful medieval generalship?

Source B.22
Of what broader medieval structure might defensive arrangements for this Edwardian borough appear to be a microcosm?

Source B.23
Should John de Havering's 200 marks a year be seen as an outright 'salary' for his custody of Caernarfon Castle? Mr Rowlands has described the castle, or '*bastide*', boroughs as the 'cutting-edge of a new colonial settlement'. What are the characteristics that can be cited as evidence of their colonial nature?

Source B.24
Master James seems to have been worried about the future in the aftermath of Madog's rebellion. What evidence can Beaumaris Castle itself offer as to the validity of his long-term fears for north Wales?

Source B.25
This letter is one of several that emanated from the north Wales boroughs after the murder of Henry de Shaldeford, the royal minister in north Wales, by Welshmen on 14 February 1345. Other instances of attacks by the Welsh on English *burgesses* and officials are rehearsed. Are

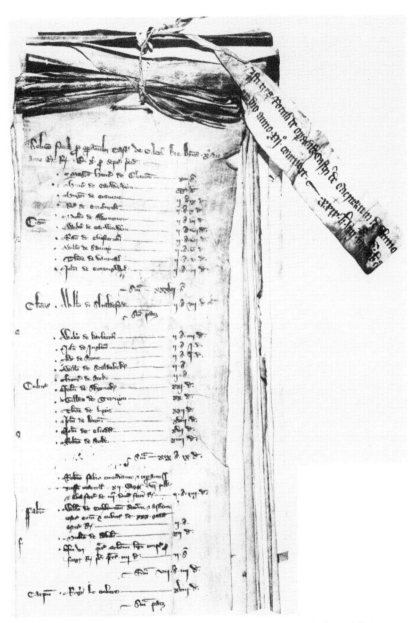

Payments to building workers at Caernarfon Castle, 1316–17. (*Source: Public Record Office.*)

the reflections on the boroughs' early years contained in these letters valid as evidence of their real state throughout the period from the 1280s to the Glyndŵr revolt in 1400?

Discussion

In one respect at least the historian of the Edwardian conquest of Wales is exceptionally fortunate. He has far more ample and precise documentation than for any earlier war in the history of medieval Europe. During the thirteenth century England became a truly bureaucratic country, in other words a state dominated by clerks and the written word. Every governmental command was written down (B.18–B.21) and detailed accounts kept of every item of expense (B.7). The historian is the beneficiary of this cult of written evidence. It means that he can give his account of Edward I's Welsh campaigns much more precision and a much richer texture than for any earlier royal expeditions. You might have noticed that many of the sources (B.2, B.9, B.12, B.17–B.19, B.21) come from the *Calendar of Welsh Rolls*. That is in itself of great significance. From 1277 Edward I decided that Wales was sufficiently important to have its own separate chancery rolls; that is a measure of the significance he attached to Wales. Edward also initiated major searches of earlier records relating to Wales in order to bolster his case and to show that he was in the right (as he saw it).

Such a wealth of documentation can, paradoxically, in itself be a danger. The historian relies on evidence. If the evidence is overwhelmingly English in its provenance, is he in danger of telling the story too much from an English angle? This is particularly true about the military aspect of the conquest where there is no Welsh parallel to the detailed English instructions on raising troops (B.1, B.19), commercial blockades (B.5), military strategy (B.12), supplies (B.18) and craftsmen (B.20, B.21). We also tend to see the aftermath of conquest largely through English eyes, as in the foundation charters of boroughs (B.22) or the nervous twitches of commanders and English settlers (B.24, B.25).

Fortunately, the balance can be rectified to some degree, as the sources show. The native Welsh chronicle (B.3, B.4) gives us a brief glimpse of the Welsh view of events. You will notice (B.4) how it interprets Llywelyn's visit to London after his defeat in 1277 as an 'invitation'. Would you regard this as an example of euphemism, just as suspected criminals nowadays are said 'to be helping the police with their inquiries'? Significantly the native Welsh chronicle is effectively abandoned after 1282; there was simply no Welsh story to tell. You can see why in the famous quotation from the elegy on Llywelyn (B.16). Poetry, especially conventional court poetry, is a notoriously difficult source for the historian, but do you think that it reaches parts of the historical memory which other sources cannot reach? Perhaps the most valuable insights we have into the Welsh side of the story are provided in the communal statements (B.8, B.13) and in Llywelyn's own declaration (B.10). Such statements must, of course, be treated with caution, but you might ask yourself how they help the historian to build up a more balanced picture of the issues behind the conquest. How would you balance Edward I's view of 'the evil deeds committed by the Welsh' (B.17) against the Welsh assertion that the English 'took their laws away from them'(B.13)? Do you get some insight from these sources into the English state propaganda machine at work (B.1, B.2, B.9)? Part of the fascination of this subject, as the sources show, is that the documentation, while, as always, less — and less well-balanced — than the historian would wish it to be, is sufficiently rich and diverse to allow us to see the issues in the round, rather than taking up a polarized pro-English or pro-Welsh position.

The Governance of Edwardian Wales

LLINOS BEVERLEY SMITH

The word governance, when it is used in relation to the reign of
Edward I, is a term which demands careful definition and
understanding. To govern in the medieval period meant to
exercise the powers and rights of lordship in several important
ways. Not only did the power of lordship entail the right to
control and to regulate, but it also involved the right to hold
courts of law and to exercise judicial functions. In any study of
governance, therefore, the lord's judicial system will loom large
because it was the prime agent of government. Indeed, during
the time of Edward I and throughout the medieval period, the
lord's courts of justice would enjoy powers which might
nowadays be distributed amongst several offices and public
bodies. A good illustration is the kind of business which came
before the court known as the turn, an organ presided over by
the *sheriff* in the king's lands and in the lordships where such a
C.1   court is known to have been held, by the lord's steward (C.1).
At the turn, which was held twice a year, representatives of the
communities were required to report breaches of a multitude of
varied regulations, ranging from serious matters such as treason
and those which touched the Crown and royal dignity, to those
concerning the taking of pigeons from dovecotes and the use of
illegal measurements. To exercise judicial powers was also to
enjoy the income and revenue which such powers gave to the
lord. Fines and *amercements* from trespasses, the sale of writs to
initiate actions in the courts would all find their way into the
lord's coffers and the safeguarding of good order and peace
within his dominions would obviously be a matter of financial
concern to his administration. Yet it would be wrong to

Thirteenth-century sculpture believed to be the head of the youthful Edward I. (*Source: Dean and Chapter of Westminster.*)

imagine that the needs of law and order would invariably rank high in the lord's priorities. Sometimes, for instance, the lord's desire to augment his income might run counter to the demands of effective government. It was possible for a man convicted of theft, a crime frequently punishable by death, to compound with his lord by paying a fine 'in order to redeem his life', a practice which would yield a useful sum of money to the lord but which would do nothing to lessen the danger of thefts and larcenies within the land. This is why historians sometimes speak of 'the limited scope of government' and it is why we need to be aware not only of the amplitude of judicial powers wielded by the lord but also of the effective narrowness of such powers of government.

The government of Wales in the reign of Edward I was divided and fragmented among a great number who exercised such powers of lordship. Though the statute enacted by the King in 1284, known as the Statute of Rhuddlan or the Statute of Wales, suggests that its contents would comprehend the whole of Wales, this was in fact not so. Despite its resonant

C.2   preamble (C.2), which claims that 'the land of Wales with its inhabitants' previously subject to Edward by *feudal* right had now been transferred to the king's direct governance, careful examination of the document's contents and the use made of it in the later medieval period shows clearly that the statute was not concerned with the whole of Wales but rather with the king's lands alone. These were the royal counties of Caernarfon, Merioneth, Anglesey and Flint, newly created in 1284, each placed in the charge of a *sheriff*, who, like his English counterpart, was to be the chief financial officer of the shire answering for the shire's revenues and the chief judicial officer of the county, presiding at sessions of the county court. In addition, the *sheriff* would preside twice a year at the turn, a court whose scope and function has already been outlined. The counties were entirely novel creations and indeed, it is the setting up of counties and 'the planting of *sheriffs*' in Wales which appeared to contemporary observers as the statute's most

C.3   notable feature (C.3). But the king also retained some features of the Welsh administrative system such as the native *commote* (*cwmwd*) which, with its court and its *bailiff*, continued to fulfil a crucial function for much of the medieval period. The two royal counties of south Wales, namely Cardiganshire and Carmarthenshire, already in existence before 1284, are briefly mentioned in the enactment, but the statute was not concerned with the details of their administration and it is unlikely that its provisions were ever enforced there until after the *union legislation* of 1536. The Crown lands in Wales, however, were in no way linked to each other in administrative terms. The royal counties of north Wales, whose chief officer was the Justice of North Wales, the county of Flint, placed under the supervision of the Justice of Chester, and the two counties of south Wales in the care of their own chief officer were separately administered in the reign of Edward I and throughout the medieval period.

The King's share of the land of Wales in 1284 was, though substantial, nevertheless a relatively small proportion of the country's total extent. The greater part consisted of lordships held of the crown by members of powerful baronial dynasties, known as the lords of the March of Wales. Many of the lordships, such as those major entities of Glamorgan and Pembroke, dated from the very earliest period of Norman penetration. Edward was to add still further to their number by the creation of new lordships, such as Denbigh, Ruthin, Bromfield and Yale, and Chirk, which were created anew in the wake of conquest out of native Welsh *cantrefs* (*cantrefi*) and *commotes*, and bestowed upon those of his loyal adjutants who C.4 had participated with him in his campaigns in Wales (C.4). These lordships, possessing many important *franchises* and liberties, were essentially governed by the command of their individual lords, and their administrative structure, as well as the precise forms of governance employed, differed considerably from one another. Glamorgan, for instance, with its county and *sheriff*, *seigneurial* and not royal institutions, and its complex administrative structure, contrasted with the lordship of Chirk, which was a somewhat artificial assemblage of three of the *commotes* of the thirteenth-century principality of Powys Fadog. There were, however, some common features, chief of which was the high degree of independence and autonomy from the royal administration enjoyed by their lords which made of each lordship virtually a 'kingdom in itself'. In many important respects, therefore, Wales continued to be, even after its conquest by Edward I, a mosaic of small units with no acknowledged unifying institution to bind the several parts together.

Yet, disparate and fractionalized as was the administrative structure of Edwardian Wales, there were agencies at work which helped impose a measure of unity and cohesion. The first was the king's own person, and it was from the institutions of royal government that the administrative unity of Wales would eventually derive in 1536. For his part, Edward I, shortly after his final victory, embarked on a triumphant progress through the land of Wales, a journey which brought him into powerful Marcher lordships such as those of Gower and Glamorgan, whose lords, within a very few years, would be amongst the most strenuous upholders of Marcher dignity. Similarly, the King emphasized his role as the fount of justice and pronounced himself 'sovereign lord' who would 'do right to all such as will complain'. Edward could also deal harshly and in masterful fashion with the lords of the March. Though he stopped short of undermining their privileges and did nothing permanently to weaken their great immunities, he could, nevertheless, assert the dignity of the Crown in the March of Wales. Two of the greatest *Marcher lords, Humphrey de Bohun*, Earl of Hereford and lord of Brecon, and *Gilbert de Clare*, Earl of Gloucester and lord of the mighty lordship of Glamorgan, were brought to task, even briefly imprisoned, and their lordships confiscated for a time. In this instance, royal intervention had been prompted by a particularly violent episode involving the two lords. The men of *Gilbert de Clare*, though specifically forbidden to do so by royal injunction, had gone into the lordship of Brecon 'with a banner of the earl's arms displayed' and had plundered and robbed within the lordship, an attack which was followed by retaliatory action on the part of the lord of Brecon. Edward, justifying his intervention by his responsibility to uphold the 'king's estate and right and for the conservation of the dignity of the crown and of his peace' was answered by *Gilbert de Clare*'s assertion of the age-old right of *Marcher lords* to go to war with one another 'according to the usage and custom of the March' (C.5). Yet, inter-lordship disputes were not always conducted in

C.5

such flamboyant fashion and by recourse to arms. For institutions had evolved which helped to counter the practical difficulties which had arisen from the fragmentation of government. Chief of these was the meetings at the frontiers of lordships, at which *seigneurial* officers and members of the several communities might be present, solemn occasions which dealt, among numerous concerns, with the extradition of wrongdoers and with serious problems such as cattle-stealing. It was to such 'days of the March' that Richard fitz Alan, lord of Oswestry and Clun, referred in 1293 when he maintained that by custom, barons of the March of Wales between whom there was discord, ought to meet at a certain place where the dispute could
C.6   be resolved by friends of both parties (C.6).

The Statute of Wales, drafted and enacted according to its preamble 'for the honour and praise of God and of Holy
C.2   Church, and to the advancement of justice' (C.2) and with due respect for native laws and customs, was, above all else, a practical working document. It outlined the *curial* framework of the principality of North Wales, provided examples of the writs to be used in actions concerning land and in personal actions such as debt, covenant and trespass and described in detail the processes to be followed when such actions were pleaded in court. But it is possible to deduce from the technical, legal content of the statute some of the principles which informed the king's written command. For instance, the statute does not discriminate against the king's Welsh subjects but extends its
C.2   provisions to 'all his subjects of his land of Snowdon' (C.2). Some of its provisions also reflect the great period of legal reform which had distinguished the reign of Edward I in England and some of the writs and processes introduced into Gwynedd benefited from the scrutiny of the king's legal experts and the improvements made by them to some aspects of English common law. The statute, in several important respects, cut across native laws and customs. Criminal law, for instance was to be the law of England and the statute finds no place for existing Welsh methods of punishing arson, theft and murder
C.7   (C.7). In the same way women were, for the first time, allowed to inherit land in the absence of male heirs, though this was contrary to Welsh law which did not allow land to descend to

C.8   females (C.8), and Welshwomen were granted a *dower* of land,
       amounting to an entitlement to a third of a deceased husband's
C.9   landed estate (C.9). But in other respects Edward allowed Welsh
       law to continue. Inheritances, for instance, were to remain
       partible according to the laws and customs of Wales though the
       king also decreed that bastards might not inherit along with
C.8   legitimate sons (C.8); certain processes of Welsh law relating to
       personal actions were also retained by the king at the request of
       the people of his lands. Though in course of time the
       inadequacies of the statute became apparent, it is a document of
       considerable craftsmanship and skill. Indeed, by the fourteenth
       century, the conqueror's statute came to be regarded as a charter
       which safeguarded the rights of the inhabitants of the king's
       lands and protected them against capricious and corrupt
       officials.

       Yet, despite the measured and statesmanlike provisions of the
       Statute of Wales, the reign of Edward I was, in later times,
       remembered as an era when punitive and oppressive measures
       were enacted against the Welsh. Acting upon the right which
       the King had reserved to himself in the Statute of Wales to
       modify its provisions as was expedient for the security of his
C.10   lands (C.10), Edward introduced a series of ordinances which
       placed serious restrictions upon those of Welsh nationality.
       Though undated in their surviving form, these measures almost
       certainly belong to the year 1295 and represent the govern-
       ment's responses to the rebellion which had recently engulfed
       many areas of the country. Among their main provisions were
       those clauses which forbade the Welsh to purchase lands and
       tenements in the walled towns of Wales, those such as
       Caernarfon and Conwy built in conjunction with the great
       castles of the conquest. Nor were the Welsh allowed to dwell
       within their precincts. Other clauses prohibited Welshmen from
       marketing their wares outside the official market towns and
       attempted to prevent public gatherings or congregations except
C.11   for those specifically licensed by the king's ministers (C.11). The
       legal arrangements outlined in the statute were, it is true, left
       untouched but there can be no doubt that a repressive and
       retributive chord was struck in royal policy towards the Welsh.
       It may be that, as some have suggested, the character of

Rhuddlan Castle. (*Source: Cadw: Welsh Historic Monuments. Crown Copyright.*)

Edward's governance changed during the last decade or so of his reign as the monarch, weighed down by deepening crises within his realm, by the burdens of war with France and Scotland and by rebellion in Wales, became more vindictive and vengeful in his attitudes. Yet, the same tendencies to distinguish and discriminate between those of Welsh and those of English nationality may be discerned in some of the Marcher lordships. In the lordship of Bromfield and Yale bestowed by Edward upon John Warenne, Earl of Surrey, in 1282, distinctions were made between those who held their lands by native Welsh tenure and the settler families of English extraction who enjoyed English land law. Indeed, the lord of Bromfield and Yale promulgated his own version of the Statute of Wales within his lordship where the royal enactment, borrowed almost in its entirety and proclaimed in the lord's name, was nevertheless modified in several important respects. For instance, the writ of *dower*, given by the king to all women in the Crown lands of north Wales irrespective of national status, was in Bromfield and Yale reserved to Englishwomen alone (C.12). Distinction and diversity, no less than statesmanlike conciliation characterized the policies of government in Wales in the wake of its final conquest.

C.12

So far our attention has been focused upon the written commands of those who wielded authority in Wales and the principles which informed their rule. Yet in our analysis of Edwardian governance, it would be quite wrong to neglect the voice of the governed. Though in England the king had, on several occasions, summoned representatives of shires and boroughs to his parliaments, Welsh communities were not so requested to attend the great assemblies of the realm. But there is ample evidence which shows that king and *Marcher lords* alike were constrained to heed the demands and grievances of the tenantry of their lands. Shortly after the death of Llywelyn ap Gruffudd the mechanisms of community petition were evidently set in motion as the men of Gwynedd presented their complaints to Edward and recounted the misgovernance of their native prince. The statute of 1284 likewise emphasizes at several points the King's willingness to enact measures at the behest of the men of the principality while, after the rebellion of

1294, the King commanded each of the royal counties of the north west, in words reminiscent of those used to summon representatives of the communities of England to Parliament, to send *proctors* armed with full powers to discuss certain

C.13 important matters with the Justice of North Wales (C.13). Similarly, the allegedly oppressive behaviour of royal officials in the Crown lands of north Wales, and the complaints of the tenantry, elicited a promise from the King that such grievances would be thoroughly investigated. Nor could the *Marcher lords* ignore the complaints and petitions of their tenants. In 1297, following the King's intervention, Edmund Mortimer, lord of Maelienydd, was compelled to grant to his men an extensive charter of liberties which allowed the tenantry of the lordship to take action in court against the lord's ministers and granted them rights of hunting and fishing within specified woods and rivers. Yet more comprehensive and far-reaching in its detailed provisions was the charter extracted by the English and Welsh tenants of the county of Gower from their lord, William de

C.14 Braose, in 1306 (C.14). The charter, comprising nearly fifty clauses, and given by the lord under the direction of the king's justices, at once shows the breadth of powers wielded by the lord of Gower and the ways in which those powers had been abused by de Braose to the grave disadvantage of his tenantry. Some of its clauses were concerned with the lord's judicial powers and many refer to the technical processes followed in the courts of the lordship. Other important clauses touched upon the behaviour of the lord's officials and allowed the tenants to seek restitution against their oppressive behaviour, while some of the concessions, such as those which refer to the levying of tolls, the tenants' rights of pasture, *pannage* and fuel for their own use reflect the extent of the lord's control over the economic life and the livelihood of the people of his lordship. Described as 'the most extensive ever made in a charter of liberties granted by a Welsh *Marcher lord*', and evoked even in Tudor times, the charter's concessions illustrate the ways in which the all-pervading powers of lords might be modified by the protests and demands of their tenants. It would be too much to claim that the business of governance in the reign of Edward I was comprised of a partnership between lords and community, or that the tenantry were invariably successful in effecting a check upon the excesses of *seigneurial* power. But, as time was to show, the needs of the governed were a quantity which those who exercised the rights and privileges of governance in Wales ignored at their peril.

Sources

C.1 And the *sheriff* by the oath of twelve *freeholders*, of the most discreet and lawful, or more at his discretion, shall diligently make inquiry upon the articles touching the crown and dignity of our lord the king hereunder written.

Of traitors to our lord the king and the realm, the queen and their children, and their abettors. Of thieves, manslayers, robbers, murderers, burners that make felonious burnings and their receivers and accessories. Of mascherers, that sell and buy stolen meat knowingly. Of whittawers, that is, those that whiten hides of oxen and horses, knowing that the same have been stolen, that they may not be known again. Of redubbers of stolen cloths, that turn them into a new shape, and change the old one, as making a coat or surcoat of a cloak, and the like. Of outlaws and abjurers of the realm that have returned to it. Of such as have withdrawn themselves against the coming and *eyre* of the justice and have returned after the *eyre*. Of ravishers of maids, nuns and matrons of good repute. Of treasure trove. Of turning water courses. Of hindrance, restraint and narrowing of the highway. Of walls, houses, gates, ditches and marl-pits raised and made near unto the public way, to the nuisance of the same way, and to the danger of passengers; and of them that raise and make the same. Of forgers of the money and seal of our lord the king. Of trespassers in parks and *vivaries*. Of breakers of the prison of our lord the king. Of takers of pigeons flying from dove cotes. Of those who make pound-breach that is, breaking of the inclosures wherein beasts are impounded. Of forstall, that is, of the stopping of cattle. Of hamsoken, that is, of breaking into houses. Of theftbote, that is, of taking amends for theft without leave of the king's court. Of them that do imprison any freeman whatsoever. Of usurers. Of removers and falsifiers of landmarks. Of non-observance of the *assize* of bread and beer and of breakers thereof. Of unlawful bushels, gallons and other measures. Of unlawful yards and weights and them that sell therewith. Of them that give lodgings to persons unknown for more than two nights. Of blood spilt; of hue and cry levied. Of them that shear sheep by night in the folds, and that flay them or any other beasts. Of them that take and collect by night the ears of corn in autumn and carry them away; and of all other the like trespassers. Let inquiry also be made of the rights of our lord the king withdrawn, as of custodies, wardships, marriages; *reliefs*, fees, *advowsons* of churches, if any there be; suits to the county and *commotes*; who shall have withdrawn them, and from what time; and of them that shall have taken upon them to exercise royalties without warrant, as gallows, fines for breach of the *assize* of bread and beer; plea of vetitum namium; and other the like rights which specially and by prerogative belong to the crown of our Lord the king.

(Articles of the sheriff's turn from the Statute of Wales, 1284, I. Bowen, *The Statutes of Wales*, London, 1908, pp.6–7.)

C.2   Edward, by the grace of God, king of England, lord of Ireland and duke of Aquitaine, to all his subjects of his land of Snowdon, greeting in the Lord. The Divine Providence, which is unerring in its own government, among other gifts of its dispensation, wherewith it hath vouchsafed to distinguish us and our realm of England, hath now of its favour, wholly and entirely transferred under our proper dominion, the land of Wales, with its inhabitants, heretofore subject unto us, in *feudal* right, all obstacles whatsoever ceasing; and hath annexed and united the same unto the crown of the aforesaid realm, as a member of the same body. We therefore, under the Divine will, being desirous that our aforesaid land of Snowdon and our other lands in those parts, like as all those which are subject unto our power, should be governed with due order to the honour and praise of God and of Holy Church, and to the advancement of justice, and that the people or inhabitants of those lands who have submitted themselves absolutely unto our will, and whom we have thereunto so accepted should be protected in security within our peace under fixed laws and customs, have caused to be rehearsed before us and the nobles of our realm, the laws and customs of those parts hitherto in use; which being diligently heard and fully understood, we have, by the advice of the aforesaid nobles, abolished certain of them, some thereof we have allowed, and some we have corrected; and we have likewise commanded certain others to be ordained and added thereto; and we will that these shall be from henceforth for ever steadfastly kept and observed in our land in these parts according to the form underwritten.

(Preamble to the Statute of Wales, Bowen, *Statutes of Wales*, pp. 2–3.)

C.3   Whereas the king has committed to Robert de Staundon his county of Meirionnydd and his office of *sheriff* in that county, as contained in the king's letters patent to him, the king, wishing to provide for his maintenance by reason of the newness of the office in the parts of Wales, has granted to him £40 yearly to be received at the *exchequer* of Caernarfon, for so long as he shall execute that office.

(Appointment of sheriff in the county of Meirionnydd, 1284, *Calendar of Chancery Rolls Various*, p. 283.)

C.4   Notification that the king has granted by this charter to Reginald de Grey the castle of Ruthin and the *cantref* of Dyffryn Clwyd . . . to hold as freely and wholly as other neighbouring *cantrefs* are held together with the forfeiture of men in the said *cantref* and land, doing therefore the service of three *knights' fees* for all service, custom and demand.

(Grant of the lordship of Dyffryn Clwyd to Reginald de Grey, 1282, *Calendar of Chancery Rolls Various*, p. 243.)

C.5   The jurors say upon their oath that William de Valers, Richard le Flemeng and Stephen de Cappenore, with a multitude of horsemen and footmen of the men of the earl of Gloucester, came out of the earl's land of Morgannwg with a banner of the earl's arms displayed on Friday after the Purification in the eighteenth year (3 February 1290) against the earl of Hereford's land of Brycheiniog, and entered that land for the space of two leagues beyond the place where the earl of Gloucester had erected the castle concerning which the dispute is, and robbed the land and carried the stolen goods to the earl of Gloucester's land . . . They also say that robbers and thieves of the land of Morgannwg have on many occasions entered the aforesaid land of Brycheiniog and robbed it and carried the stolen goods to the land of Morgannwg . . . And upon being asked whether the robbers had slain any of the men of the earl of Hereford, or had burnt any of the houses of the said men or had robbed any churches in the land of the earl, they say that the thieves burned a house in the land of Brycheiniog at Tiraph and broke a church called Penyderyn and took and carried away the chalice and other goods whatsoever there found . . . They also say that the total of the oxen, cows, heifers and beasts of this kind robbed is 1,070; the total of horses, plough horses and colts stolen is 50; they are wholly ignorant of the number of sheep, swine and goats . . . Being asked if the said robberies were done by the order and with the knowledge of the earl of Gloucester and if any of the goods stolen came to the profit of the earl, they say that the earl of Gloucester knew well of the three robberies made with the banner displayed, and that he had a third of the goods thus stolen as it befits the lords to have in time of war in accordance with the use and custom of the March.

(Record, 1291, of the controversy between Humphrey de Bohun, Earl of Hereford, and Gilbert de Clare, Earl of Gloucester, *Calendar of Chancery Rolls Various*, pp.337–8.)

C.6   Fulk fitz Warin complains against Richard fitz Alan, earl of Arundel, that he, in arms and with banners displayed, plundered the lands of Fulk at Whittington. Richard says that he is a baron of the *Welshry* where it is a recognized custom that the barons of those parts, whenever such a discord arises amongst them, ought to come together at a certain place, where the dispute should be settled by the friends of both parties.

(Record of a case between Fulk fitz Warin and Richard fitz Alan, 1293, *Abbreviatio Placitorum*, p.226.)

C.7   Yet so that they hold not place in thefts, larcenies, burnings, manslaughters and manifest and notorious robberies nor do by any means extend unto these; wherein we will that they shall use the laws of England as is before declared.

(Statute of Wales, Bowen, *Statutes of Wales*, p.26.)

C.8   Whereas the custom is otherwise in Wales than in England concerning succession to an inheritance inasmuch as the inheritance is *partible* among the heirs male, and from time whereof the memory of man is not to the contrary hath been *partible*, our lord the king will not have that custom abrogated; but willeth that inheritances shall remain *partible* among like heirs as it was wont to be; and partition of the same inheritance shall be made as it was wont to be made; with the exception, that bastards from henceforth shall not inherit; and also shall not have portions with the lawful heirs nor without the lawful heirs; and if it happens that any inheritance should hereafter upon the failure of heir male descend unto females, the lawful heirs of their ancestor last *seised* thereof, we will of our especial grace that the same women shall have their portions thereof to be assigned them in our court, although this be contrary to the custom of Wales before used.

(Statute of Wales, Bowen, *Statutes of Wales*, pp.25–6.)

C.9   And whereas heretofore women have not been endowed in Wales, the king granteth that they shall be endowed.

(Statute of Wales, Bowen, *Statutes of Wales*, p.24.)

C.10   And therefore we command you that from henceforth you do steadfastly observe the premises in all things. So notwithstanding that whensoever and wheresoever, and as often as it shall be our pleasure, we may declare, interpret, enlarge or diminish the aforesaid statutes and the several parts of them, according to our mere will and as to us shall seem expedient for the security of us and our land aforesaid. In witness whereof our seal hath been affixed to these presents.

Given at Rhuddlan on Sunday in Mid Lent in the twelfth year of our reign.

(Statute of Wales, Bowen, *Statutes of Wales,* pp.26–7.)

C.11   The Welsh shall not purchase lands and tenements in the English walled boroughs nor within the liberties of English boroughs and towns under pain of forfeiture of the lands and tenements so purchased, and this by ordinance of the aforesaid conqueror as appears in the record.

It was ordained by the lord Edward the conqueror that no Welshman should dwell in the walled towns nor hold *burgages* but should be removed by the mayors and *bailiffs* of the said towns. And that no Welshman should carry arms within the walled or English towns under penalty of loss or forfeiture of the arms and imprisonment at the lord's will.

It was ordained by the conqueror that no Welshman should make any transaction outside the market towns nor should brew beer for sale, under pain or forfeiture of merchandise and imprisonment or make redemption.

It was ordained by the lord Edward, conqueror of Wales, that no congregations should be made by the Welsh in north Wales to make agreements or suggestions unless by royal licence or unless the chief ministers of the parts be present.

(Supplementary Ordinances, probably *c.*1295, H. Ellis (ed.), *The Record of Caernarvon*, London, 1838, pp.131–2.)

C.12   Now *dower* will be discussed, because according to Welsh tenure, that is to say, *gafaelion*, by the custom of these parts no woman shall be endowed of the land and inheritance of her husband. But if her husband hold acres of land by military service or by charter or by English tenure then according to the law of England, *dower* is reckoned to her and she shall have *dower*.

(The 'Arundel' version of the Statute of Wales, British Library, Add.MS 10,013, f.5v.)

C.13   It is found in various records that diverse homicides, robberies,

and thefts have been committed by evildoers and disturbers of
the peace in various places within the county of Caernarfon; and
complaints have been frequently made to the Justice by various
aggrieved persons of those parts. Wherefore the Justice, for the
preservation of the peace has caused to come before him all the
better and worthier Welshmen of the county having full powers
for the community of the whole county to ordain and establish
with the council of the said Justice an appropriate remedy in this
matter.

(Supplementary Ordinances, *The Record of Caernarvon*, p.132.)

C.14   To all the faithful of Christ who see or hear this present writing,
from William de Breosa, lord of the honours of Brembre and
Gower, greeting.

Know all that we have granted and by this our present charter
confirmed for us and our heirs and assigns, to all the abbots,
priors, *Knights Hospitallers* and *Templars*, knights, free tenants
and the tenants and men of these, whether English or Welsh,
living within the area of our English county of Gower or
holding land therein, all and singular the liberties hereinafter
noted, to have and to hold to us and our successors, heirs and
assigns for ever.

We will and grant that all our officials in the English county
should answer all true complaints made about them without a
solemn narration of the wrongs and injustices perpetrated by
the officials. Compensation, restitution and amendment should
be judged according to custom for the crime, the amount to be
decided by the consideration of the county. This should be fully
executed.

Neither we nor any of our officials shall take from henceforth
corn, fish or any kind of animals or any other chattels of the said
men, without immediately paying the price thereof, unless we
are allowed a postponement by the agreement and will of the
seller.

In addition we will and grant for us and our heirs for ever that
our *chancery* in Gower should always be held openly and should
be ready for all to petition for writs without any difficulty.

No more than seven pence should be given for each writ. If a plaintiff obtain a writ and is dissatisfied with the form of the writ granted to him by the *chancery*, another writ should be made for him according to his direction at his own risk, as long as it seems within the law, and a transcript thereof should be given to the plaintiff for one penny.

Also each free man should have the nests of falcons, sparrow-hawks and other birds in his woods and lands, and likewise a swarm of bees and honey found in his woods without any claim.

We grant to the aforesaid men that they should freely pasture all their pigs in all our woods in Gower Uwchloed, apart from the wood of Predewen, without paying *pannage* dues or any other dues.

We further grant to our men aforesaid that they should have the coal-mine in Gelliwastad with no hindrance from us, our heirs or any of our officials, in order to supply all their necessities, but without selling any coal.

(Charter granted by William de Braose to the lordship of Gower, 1306. G. T. Clark, *Cartae et Alia Munimenta quae ad Domininium de Glamorgancia pertinent*, III, 2nd edition, 1910, pp.990–8.)

Debating the Evidence

The documentation relating to Wales during the period immediately after the conquest inevitably deals largely with the consequences of that conquest. The creation of a structure of government and administration, the establishment of authority at grass-roots level and the securing of the compliance of the governed were no mean task. It generated a mass of documentation, of necessity slanted towards the views of the Crown officials who initiated it. The seminal document was the Statute of Wales, 1284, which created the political framework for the principality. Later, supplementary ordinances provide an essential corollary to the Statute.

Source C.1
Dr Smith has described both the apparent breadth of jurisdiction

enjoyed by the lordship courts and the practical limitations that constrained them. How can the records of courts such as the *sheriff's* turn provide us with insights into various aspects of medieval everyday life?

Source C.2
How far does the preamble to the Statute of Rhuddlan appear to suggest a 'colonial' regime in Wales, under which the native Welsh would be subject to discrimination? How does the document summarize the difference between the principality's previous status in respect of the English Crown and the new position? Does the document herald a 'clean sweep' of Welsh administrative and legal processes in the wake of the conquest?

Source C.3
Dr Smith's text shows how the crucial office of *sheriff*, as the agent of royal power, was in some cases grafted on to the established framework of a *cantref* or *cwmwd*. A study of William Rees's *Historical Atlas of Wales* or Melville Richards's *Welsh Administrative and Territorial Units* will show which native Welsh administrative units survived the transition to English rule. What difficulties do you think might be faced by a new *sheriff* arriving in a *cantref* such as Meirionnydd in Gwynedd in 1284?

Source C.4
What, if anything, in this document implies a novel form of tenure in Dyffryn Clwyd which would distinguish royal grantees and their rights from other lords in the region? What demonstrates the military basis of English control at this time?

Source C.5
Bearing in mind that *Humphrey de Bohun* and *Gilbert de Clare* had been among the most determined opponents of Llywelyn ap Gruffudd in the Welsh Marches, how far was there any inconsistency in their cavalier attitude to the 'king's peace' as reflected in this document compared with their resistance to Llywelyn before 1282?

Source C.6
What parallel might be drawn between the arbitration procedure of the Welsh March as outlined in this document and a practice employed by Llywelyn ap Gruffudd outlined in a document in Section B?

Source C.7

The section of the Statute of Wales in which this passage occurs emphasizes that 'the people of Wales have besought us [the King]' to allow the use of Welsh law to try civil cases before 'good and lawful men of the neighbourhood, chosen by consent of parties'. The King granted this 'for the common peace and quiet of our aforesaid people'. Why, then, should the King have been determined to apply English legal processes in criminal cases? In view of the fact that the penal code under Welsh law comprised, for the most part, a schedule of differentiated rates of compensation for victims and their kin according to their status and the nature and circumstances of the offence, why should Edward I have observed that many of the Welsh laws were 'contrary to the Ten Commandments'?

Source C.8

How far does the decision to retain *partible inheritance* of land appear to have been made as a result of the wishes of the people of Wales? Is there any reason why the retention of this practice might benefit royal authority and the new Edwardian lordships created after the conquest?

Source C.9

The status of women under Welsh law was very complicated. Women were allowed half the household goods in any divorce settlement after seven years, and a woman's son by a non-member of the tribe or *cenedl* could claim inheritance by virtue of his mother. A woman could not inherit land in her own right, even in the absence of direct male heirs. In what sort of situation might the previous legal situation have caused problems under post-Conquest conditions?

Source C.10

What developments might:
a) put the more conciliatory aspects of the new regime under a severe strain and prompt the Crown to 'enlarge or diminish the aforesaid statutes and the several parts of them'?
b) undermine the Crown's efforts to appear to 'do right to all such as will complain' in the principality?

Source C.11

To what specific events between 1284 and 1295 can these supplementary royal ordinances be seen as a reaction? The new *bastide* towns, or castle boroughs, within the principality had largely been developed as plantations or colonies of English *burgesses* in the wake of the conquest. Even the old-established borough of Rhuddlan had been reconstituted after 1277, with an English borough being established on a separate site from the older town. What might the 1295 ordinances imply about the towns during the decade since the conquest? What areas of research might yield further information on this point?

Source C.12

The term '*dower*' (not to be confused with 'dowry' — the property a bride brings with her into wedlock) refers to a widow's due share of her late husband's property. It was an English legal concept applying to land. In what sense, then, were the framers of the 1284 statute correct in saying that women had no *dower* under Welsh law?

Source C.13

In the writ summoning Edward I's 'Model Parliament' of 1295 these famous words, of Roman origin, appeared: 'That which touches all should be approved by all.' The principality of Wales sent no representative to that parliament, and except for two of Edward II's parliaments, none to any other before 1536. What degree of involvement at local level in the maintenance of law and order does this ordinance suggest? Would it appear to be a consultative operation prior to executive action by the Justice, or a 'hands-on' process which involved the Welsh themselves in preserving order? What features of the post-conquest regime in the principality and of medieval lordship in general would have made it difficult for the Crown to maintain close supervision?

Source C.14

The things William de Braose promised to refrain from doing in future are cited here as indications of what he had been doing in the past. What problems can arise in 'working backwards' in this way from a particular piece of evidence to broader conclusions about general medieval practice? What does this charter mean when it refers to the 'English county of Gower'?

Discussion

All the sources in this section are official documents; they look at the problems of governance and authority through the eyes of the governors rather than the governed. This is not an unusual situation in history. Governments, after all, are much more likely to be the keepers of records than private individuals. But the problem this poses for the historian in a country such as Wales after the Edwardian conquest, where the native population is almost completely silent in the surviving historical records (but see Section E) and where a barrier of language compounded the problem of comprehension, is particularly acute.

Yet the historian must make a virtue of his necessity; and in any case the problems and attitudes of governments in coping with a native, newly-conquered society are themselves fascinating. The key document here is the Statute of Wales; there are no less than six excerpts from it in these sources (C.1, C.2, C.7–C.10). You might ask why Edward I issued such a statute; after all, no earlier ruler on conquering a country had felt the need to issue a great statute. Part of the answer lies in the preamble (C.2). That talks of 'due order', 'the advancement of justice', the need for 'fixed laws and customs'. Why should a conqueror need to explain himself and to whom was he explaining himself — to God, to the English political community, to the Welsh? As so often with statutes, it is not only the rhetoric of the preambles which helps to explain the legislator's intention; the small print of the individual clauses is equally significant. Does the introduction of the *sheriff*, the shire (C.3) and the turn (C.1) indicate that Edward I felt that the Welsh would benefit from a dose of English administrative medicine? You will note that there is an ambivalence in his attitude to Welsh law. He says (C.2) that he has reviewed and amended it. Why, then, does he allow Welsh land division and inheritance to survive (C.8), but gives the thumbs down to Welsh criminal law (C.7) and rules out the rights of illegitimate children (C.8)? And was Edward I an early supporter of women's rights with his insistence that women should enjoy dower (C.9) and be permitted to inherit land (C.8)? It is important to read between the lines of statutes and see what they say about the legislator's view of the world. Does that suggest that the Statute of Wales will say more about a thirteenth-century English king and his advisers than about Wales?

Laws are one thing; life is another. Some of the other sources suggest that life was not quite as tidy as the Statute of Wales would suggest.

What, for example, do you make of the disjunction between the Statute and the impression of utter disorder and lawlessness in the March of Wales (C.5, C.6)? Is it a real disjunction or is it a matter of different kinds of sources, or of model and reality? Then again you might contrast the majestic and generous tones of the Statute with the paranoid and discriminatory clauses of the ordinances of 1295 (C.11). What explains the contrast between them and which gets us closer to the true feelings of the English about the Welsh? The last two documents (C.13, C.14) should also make you wonder whether there is more to the legislation than meets the eye. Did the governors after all have to listen to the governed and were some of their edicts in reality responses to community complaints? The Gower charter (C.14) takes us away from grand legislative edicts and high matters of law and administration to matters of falcons, bees, pigs and coal-mines. Were those the issues that really bothered Welshmen? You might care to compare the issues raised in the Kennington petitions (E.2, E.3, E.11, E.15–E.17, E.21) and ask whether petitions take us closer than statutes and ordinances to the world of real people.

An early twentieth-century representation of Gerald of Wales. (*Source: Cardiff City Council.*)

The Church and Monasticism in the Age of Conquest

GLANMOR WILLIAMS

In the life of Wales and all other countries of western Christendom in the thirteenth century, the Church occupied a central place. At the most mundane level it was a major landowner: its bishops and abbots were among the ruler's wealthiest and most influential *tenants-in-chief*, exercising jurisdiction over many lesser figures; it was highly important as a potential source of support in money and men; and because its clergy were celibate (in theory at least) they could not create a hereditary vested interest. Clerics also enjoyed a near-monopoly of formal education, numbering amongst them some of the best-trained minds of the age; indispensable to lay rulers and magnates as weighty advisers and skilled administrators (D.1). The Church was, furthermore, the focus of profound local, regional, even quasi-national loyalties, the shrines and relics of whose saints were the external manifestations of God's covenant with His people and tokens of His favour. Finally, and in some ways most significant of all, the Church controlled all the principal thought-systems of the age. It sanctioned the exercise on earth of political, legal, and social authority, all of which were believed to derive ultimately from God; and it determined the means of salvation in the world to come (undeniably real and vivid to most folk), to which it could deny access by imposing *excommunication* and *interdict*.

The Church and religion were too important in the eyes of lay rulers to be left entirely to clerics; they believed it to be essential to get their own hands on its levers of power and influence as far as they could. But, by the same token, if the Church was so crucial to human society, it would inevitably wish to assert its

D.1

right to fulfil its mission on earth independently of lay domination. Spearheaded by a reformed papacy, which attained the zenith of its authority in the thirteenth century, clerics cherished their own elevated and awe-inspiring aspiration to bring about through the Church the rule of the Kingdom of God on earth and would not lightly allow anyone to stand in the way of its fulfilment. One of their liveliest representatives in Wales was *Giraldus Cambrensis*, who had stood up so valiantly against the King and the Archbishop of Canterbury for the rights of the see of St Davids (D.2).

D.2

These great issues came home to Wales in three main ways during the age of Edward I and Prince Llywelyn ap Gruffudd. First, the Church had, for a century or more, been an important instrument in the process of conquering Wales and, late in the thirteenth century, continued to be so. Second, there were tensions between Church and State which often cut clean across the normal pattern of hostility between Welsh and Anglo-Normans. Third, beneath these spectacular clashes at the highest levels, the Church went on performing its normal grass-roots functions of maintaining belief, worship, instruction, and social welfare.

Ever since the Norman conquest of Wales had begun late in the eleventh century, the king, *Marcher lords*, and archbishop of Canterbury had made effective use of the Church to help them overcome Welsh resistance. Having compelled bishops of Welsh dioceses regularly to acknowledge the authority of Canterbury, they continued to insist upon such obedience in the

D.3

thirteenth century (D.3). Again, they had introduced into Wales monasteries belonging to religious orders of a kind with which they were familiar, like the *Benedictines* or the *Augustinian Canons*. Such monasteries were sited in or near boroughs like Chepstow, Brecon, or Haverfordwest, which the Normans had set up to consolidate their grip on their conquests. They were usually daughter-priories of abbeys in France or England and were handsomely endowed with land formerly belonging to the native Welsh *clasau* (community churches). Most of their monks were non-Welsh in origin, alienated from the native population; and their houses were as much a part of the pattern of Norman domination as the castle and its garrison, the borough, and the lordship.

Such encroachments had not gone unchallenged and, in the thirteenth century, were still being resisted. The princes of Gwynedd made determined and successful efforts to influence the choice of bishops in the two northern dioceses, where Bishops Anian of Bangor (1267–1305/6) and Anian of St Asaph (1268–93) both owed their election to Prince Llywelyn ap Gruffudd. A number of the higher clergy in these and other Welsh dioceses were also Welsh and closely associated with native rulers. Nor were all the monasteries of Wales, particularly those of the Cistercian order, under the thumb of foreign lords. True, Cistercians had first been introduced into Wales by Normans; but a number of their monasteries, unlike those of the *Benedictines*, became completely assimilated into Welsh life. These White Monks — so-called because of the colour of the robes they wore — did not cling to the skirts of castle and borough but sought out lonely, wooded, and undeveloped locations, where they set a splendid example as advanced agriculturalists and expert sheep-breeders and cattle-raisers. Their holy life, strict discipline, attention to education, and patronage of literature won them a unique place in the affections of Welsh princes and people. How closely they became associated with patriotic loyalties and princely aspirations may readily be seen from the *Brut y Tywysogyon* (*The Chronicle of the* **D.4** *Princes*)which they were responsible for compiling (D.4). From their ranks the Welsh rulers recruited highly-trained servants and counsellors.

The newer orders of friars, the *Dominicans* and *Franciscans*, who first arrived in Wales in the 1240s, proved just as much of an asset to the country as the Cistercians. Whereas the monks had withdrawn from the world, the crying need of the thirteenth century was for the friars to plunge into it to follow their vocation. Only thus could they proclaim to the populace their special message: the teaching of the Church, its strictures on excessive wealth, and its condemnation of heresy. Their particular instruments for the purpose were the confessional and the sermon, which meant placing increased emphasis on the Welsh language in preaching, literature and penitential discipline. Having quickly become the most learned among the clergy, the friars were looked upon by the pope as his principal

D.5

agents for religious renewal and reform. They, too, provided willing representatives and diplomats for the princes (D.5). So, although the king of England and the archbishop of Canterbury exercised considerable jurisdiction over the Church and used it to promote their ends, the native rulers of Wales could also look to the Church and clergy to serve some of their purposes as well.

Those tensions which arose between Church and State could exist as easily between the clergy and princes of Wales as between the king of England and his clerics. For instance, the struggle for the independence of their diocese of St Davids was not primarily a battle between Welsh and Normans so much as a contest which arose out of the affirmation of the rights of the Church, and especially the liberties of St Davids, against king and archbishop. It was one in which the first Norman bishop of the see, Bernard, or *Gerald of Wales*, himself three parts a Norman, could take the side of St Davids. Again, Edwards I's archbishop, John Pecham, could argue for the maintenance of some of the distinctive ecclesiastical liberties of the Welsh Church against the interests and wishes of his royal

D.20

master (D.20).

The most celebrated clash between Church and State in the Wales of the period, however, was that between Prince Llywelyn and the Bishops of St Asaph and Bangor. Anian of St Asaph came of princely lineage, his mother being a second cousin to Llywelyn. A *Dominican* friar and a man of masterful and ambitious disposition, he was appointed bishop in 1268. For some years he was on good terms with Llywelyn, active as a diplomat for him in 1271–2, and, even as late as 1274, trying to compose differences between him and his brother,

D.6

Dafydd (D.6).

Friction between prince and bishop was almost bound to be generated, nevertheless. In those parts of Anian's diocese which had been under English rule before 1267, English customs favourable to the Church had been adopted in matters relating to the rights of ecclesiastical courts over wills and the punishment of clerics who broke the law. Over these issues Anian was not disposed, either by temperament or by training, to give way to Llywelyn. Being a friar, he was naturally inclined to look for support to a fellow-mendicant in the person of

Bangor Cathedral. (*Source: National Monuments Record for Wales.*)

Robert Kilwardby, Archbishop of Canterbury. Such a link was bound to be viewed with the deepest suspicion by Llywelyn, devoted son of the Church and generous patron to it though he was. He saw Anian's connection with Canterbury laying him and his subjects open to the danger of being excommunicated for political reasons. He was, moreover, a strong prince prepared to treat the Church with a heavy hand, if necessary, when pushing his state-building policies in the direction of a more unified authority.

The trouble, long brewing between the two men, came to the boil in 1273, when Bishop Anian complained to Pope Gregory X of Llywelyn's oppressive treatment of some of the Bishop's tenants. The Prince's conduct was warmly defended, on the other hand, in a reply dated 7 March 1274 and signed by the heads of the leading Cistercian abbeys of Whitland, Strata Florida, Cwm-hir, Strata Marcella, Conwy, Cymer, and Valle

D.7   Crucis (D.7). Even Pope Gregory seems to have been favourably enough disposed towards Llywelyn to order the Archbishop of Canterbury not to *excommunicate* him or his men if they were willing to appear before his commissioners in Wales. In response, Anian moved closer to Kilwardby, to whom he sent a series of complaints against Llywelyn, to which the

D.8   latter replied with a detailed defence of his actions (D.8,
D.9   D.9). Anian then raised the stakes by bidding directly for
D.10   Edward I's support (D.10). The King's alert eye was quick to spot a potentially valuable ally at a time when his own relations with Llywelyn were deteriorating. He promptly offered Anian

D.11   the 'ancient liberties' of his diocese on 8 November 1275 (D.11). To show his gratitude for such favour, Anian attended the royal council of 1276, at which Llywelyn was declared a rebel and military preparations against him were decided upon.

The politico-military crisis confronting Llywelyn in 1276–7 provided Anian and his *chapter* with a not-to-be-missed opening

D.12   to draw up a long list of complaints (D.12). They condemned Llywelyn's efforts to control the election of bishops, his attempts to tax the clergy, his insistence on bringing clerics to trial in secular courts, and his refusal to allow church courts to try questions relating to sacrilege, marriage disputes, or wills. Neither Llywelyn nor Anian could have been said to have right wholly on his side, but on balance Welsh practice favoured the Prince rather than the Bishop. Llywelyn was, however, too hard-pressed elsewhere to take a determined stand and was forced to concede to the Bishop most of the issues in dispute. Despite that concession, in the course of the military operations of 1276–7 Anian ranged himself on the English side, and he and his canons were taken under royal protection.

Once Edward had successfully concluded his campaign, he rewarded Anian and removed much of St Asaph diocese from Llywelyn's rule. For some years afterwards Anian maintained reasonably good relations with the King. As late as 1281 he joined in a petition to the Pope seeking permission for Edward to move the cathedral from St Asaph to Rhuddlan. At the same time, though, he urged the Pope not to allow the transfer until the King had given a further guarantee to respect the liberties of the diocese (D.13), which had been infringed when his officials removed actions to his courts from the bishop's. In the spring of 1282, when the Welsh rebelled against Edward, St Asaph cathedral was accidentally destroyed by English soldiers. In a towering rage, Anian *excommunicated* them and fled from his diocese. He refused point-blank to *excommunicate* the Welsh — the only bishop in the whole kingdom who would not do so.

The Bishop of Bangor — another Anian — also clashed with Llywelyn. Being nearer to the Prince than his namesake of St Asaph, he came under severer pressure from him. Although he was a much less pugnacious character, he found himself in an increasingly intolerable position. Writing to Edward in 1277 he declared that he loved his people and his prince but would do so only 'with a good conscience, saving the honour of God and the Church'. Although he was Llywelyn's confessor and 'could not stir a foot except under the prince's power', he dared to *excommunicate* him (D.14). As soon as war broke out he fled to St Albans for refuge and was given the King's protection. Returning to Bangor after the conclusion of the Treaty of Aberconwy, Anian found himself sorely ill at ease. Llywelyn rejoiced at the wartime losses suffered by the Bishop and continued to infringe the liberties of the Church (D.15). He justified his actions by opposing the *Law of Hywel Dda* to that of the Church — greatly to the indignation of Pecham.

Margin notes: D.13, D.14, D.15

Valle Crucis. (*Source: National Monuments Record for Wales.*)

Gradually, relations between prince and bishop appeared to improve somewhat. At all events, Pecham wrote to say how pleased he was by the agreement amicably arrived at between them. Any friendship that may have blossomed, however, could not stand the strain of a fresh outbreak of war. In 1282 Anian again went over to the English side. It is significant that his cathedral at Bangor was reported by the Welsh chronicler to be the place where the conspiracy of late 1282 was hatched against

D.16   Llywelyn (D.16), though it is not known how many laymen and how many clerics were implicated in it, or who they were. What is certain is that, by 1282, Llywelyn's policies had driven a wedge between him and the native leaders of the Church. In order to uphold its privileges, they had felt obliged to seek the friendship and protection of the English Crown. When they returned to their dioceses after the war, they did so as agents of Edward I and by his favour.

Beneath all the struggles for power at the top and the manœuvrings of princes and prelates, the Church continued to engage in its essential task of trying to save people's souls and conducting its pastoral care as best it could in a turbulent and uncertain age. Parish, rural deanery, archdeaconry, diocese, and province, all looked ultimately for leadership to the Pope as God's Vicar on earth and the fountain-head of the Church. To Rome they directed their requests, petitions, and suits, and from Rome there came a constant stream of advice, exhortation, and instruction for the guidance of the local and national churches

D.17   (D.17). Similarly, representatives of the Cistercian abbeys travelled regularly to meetings of the chapter-general of their order at the mother-house of Cîteaux to keep in touch with all the other Cistercian houses and tread a common path of spiritual discipline and endeavour. In all cathedrals and monasteries, and on a lesser scale in parish churches, a regular round of ordered worship and *supplication* was maintained in the common language of the western Church — Latin. On Sundays and holy days, and in religious houses every day, mass was offered at all the altars as a sacrifice intended to benefit the living and the dead. The Church and its priesthood duly commemorated Christmas, Easter, Whitsun and other festivals of the Christian calendar and the principal milestones of most human lives:

birth, marriage, and death. Couples were married, children christened and confirmed, the sick comforted, and the dead buried. Pilgrims were encouraged to wend their laborious way to shrines and sacred places as distant as Jerusalem and Rome, as well as to St Davids, Bardsey, Strata Florida, or Holywell, and many other sites, far and near. There they venerated the saints, and with the help of the holy relics sought the health of their own souls and bodies and the welfare of their animals and crops. Further help for pilgrims, the sick and disabled was provided at hospitals founded by clerics (D.18) and in the infirmaries of the monasteries, which also furnished hospitality for the traveller and alms for the poor.

D.18

In the Church courts, canon law — the law of the Church — was enforced; erring priests were corrected and disciplined, and lay men and women punished for their moral failings. The Church also tried to guarantee the sanctity of contracts and agreements by ensuring that they were sworn to at the grave of a saint or on holy relics, thus threatening to invoke heavenly wrath if the undertaking were broken. Priests were much exercised, too, as arbitrators and peace-makers in the many feuds and quarrels of the time. A large part of contemporary education was provided by the Church. Cathedrals, monasteries, and the larger churches conducted schools, from which a handful of the brightest boys might go on to the universities. Not merely might they proceed to Oxford and Cambridge, but also to Paris, Bologna, and other major European centres of learning; just as John Wallensis ('the Welshman') went to Oxford to become Regent-Master to the *Franciscans* and later to Paris, where he was known as *arbor vitae* ('tree of life'). At the monastic *scriptoria* the scribes painstakingly copied such valuable manuscripts as the Book of Taliesin and the White Book Mabinogion and stored them in their libraries. Monasteries were frequently important centres of intellectual, literary, and historical activity; and it was Strata Florida, with the help of other Cistercian houses, that was responsible for compiling the chronicle, *Brut y Tywysogyon*, which recorded the history of Wales and the feats of its princes. The clergy, too, must have had a considerable hand in commissioning, and perhaps translating into Welsh from Latin, a considerable body of religious literature found in manuscripts like Peniarth MS 14 and 16. They included Welsh versions of part of St Matthew's Gospel, the Lord's Prayer, and the Creed, and were intended to help the unlearned mass of parish clergy who had no more than a limited knowledge of Latin. Some of the friars were particularly interested in literature, and one of them, Madog ap Gwallter, was responsible for one of the most charming of all

D.19   Welsh religious poems (D.19).

Edward's final campaigns of 1282–3 were as damaging to the Church and its ministers as to laymen. When the wars were over, Archbishop Pecham was greatly perturbed by the possible outcome for the Welsh Church and urged the King to preserve its ancient liberties. He warned him to protect Welsh clerics against the 'carnally wise but spiritually foolish' royal officials lest the increase of his honour should 'turn to the mourning of

D.20   the Church' (D.20). Edward was reluctant to give any encouragement to clerics whom he thought to have been nearly as rebellious as the laity; but he was experienced enough a ruler to appreciate the need to keep the Church on his side as far as possible. He therefore came to terms not only with bishops like the two Anians but also with the leading Cistercians and friars, some of whom had backed Llywelyn to the end.

Two visitations followed in 1284; the one conducted by Pecham, the other by Edward. In June Pecham proceeded from St Asaph to Bangor and on to St Davids, where he crossed swords with Bishop Bek over the rights of St Davids to be independent of Canterbury. He issued injunctions for the diocese and a number of monasteries and moved on to Llandaff. He was also instrumental in obtaining large sums for rebuilding and repairing war-damaged Welsh churches. In September Edward began a three-month royal progress through Wales. He restored Bishop Anian to St Asaph and rewarded the Bishop of Bangor. In a conciliatory gesture to Wales's patron saint and most famous shrine, he and his queen came to St Davids as pilgrims.

So had Edward and Pecham set the stamp of their authority

D.21   on the Welsh Church (D.21). They had made it plain that clerics no less than laymen were subjects of the king and the Church was firmly incorporated into his realm. But many Welsh clerics, like their lay brothers, clung tenaciously to their awareness of nationality and a half-submerged longing for independence. In just over a century it would resurface when they gave vent to their feelings in the Glyndŵr Rebellion.

Sources

D.1   To record in perpetuity the agreement reached in the year 1263 . . . between the lord Llywelyn son of Gruffudd, on the one part, and the lord Gruffudd son of Gwenwynwyn, on the other, namely, that the said lord Gruffudd of his own free will did *homage* for himself and his heirs in the presence of the venerable Father in God Richard, bishop of Bangor, the lords abbots of Aberconwy and Strata Florida, Brother Ieuaf of the Order of Preachers, Master David, archdeacon of Bangor, Adam, rural dean of Ardudwy, and David son of William, official of Dyffryn Clwyd . . .

(Agreement concerning homage between Llywelyn ap Gruffydd and Gruffydd ap Gwenwynwyn, 12 December 1263. J. Goronwy Edwards (ed.), *Littere Wallie*, Cardiff, 1940, p.111.)

D.2   The archdeacon [*Gerald of Wales*] was descended from both nations, from the princes of Wales and the barons of the March, yet he hated injustice in whichever nation he saw it. What could be more unjust than that that nation, founded and rooted in the faith from of old, long before the coming of the Saxons, merely because they defend their bodies, lands, and liberties against hostile people, repelling force with force, should immediately be separated from the body of Christ?

(J. Conway Davies (ed.), *Episcopal Acts Relating to Welsh Dioceses, 1066–1272*, 2 vols., Cardiff, 1946–8, p.310.)

D.3   Profession by Richard, bishop-elect of St Davids, to Richard, archbishop of Canterbury and primate of all England and to the church of Canterbury and his successors canonically appointed, of due and canonical obedience and subjection in all things, according to the decrees of the popes of Rome, the archbishop and the church of Canterbury. He will defend and maintain the same, saving his order. He confirms all the same by the subscription of his hand.

He was consecrated in the Roman *curia* and then made his profession in Christ Church, Canterbury, at the high altar, to Master William de Mortimer, then representing Archbishop Boniface.

(1256. Davies, *Episcopal Acts*, p.393.)

D.4   Y vlwydyn honno ybu varw phylip goch, abat ystrat flur; ac yny ol y doeth einyawn seis, dan yr hwn y llosges y vanachloc wedy hynny. Wedy hynny noswyl veir sanfreid y kanawd tomas esgob mynyw yr efferen gyntaf a gant yny esgobod ar yr allawr vawr yn eglwys ystrat flur. Odyna digwyl dewi y kyssegrwyt ef yn esgob yny eistedua y mynwy.

(That year [1280] died Philip Goch, abbot of Strata Florida, and after him came Einion Sais, under whom the monastery was afterwards burnt. After that on the feast of Mary (following) St Brigid, Thomas, bishop of St Davids, sang the first mass of his episcopate at the high altar of the church of Strata Florida. Then on St David's Day he was consecrated bishop of his cathedral at St Davids.)

(Thomas Jones (ed.), *Brut y Twyysogyon, Peniarth MS 20 Version*, Cardiff, 1952, p.120.)

D.5   . . . William informs the king that the Prince of Wales, his faithful and devoted *vassal*, has very great occasion of complaint if the business between him and Gruffydd ap Gwenwynwyn is further delayed . . . since the delay in the business seems to Llywelyn to run counter to the form of peace, and compulsion to restore the aforesaid goods altogether takes away his liberty . . . as William has already told the king elsewhere by word of mouth . . . William is writing these things to the king from the zeal which he has for the continuance of peace between them, in

Brut y Tywysogyon or *The Chronicle of the Princes*. (*Source: National Library of Wales.*)

order that the king may have a more certain way of answering the petitions of the prince.

(1281–2. Friar William de Merton, Warden of the Friars Minor of Llanfaes, to King Edward I. J. Goronwy Edwards, *Calendar of Ancient Correspondence Concerning Wales*, Cardiff, 1935, pp.99–100.)

D.6   To the venerable fathers in Christ by the grace of God bishops of Bangor and St Asaph, their devoted son, Llywelyn, prince of Wales, sends greeting, reverence, and honour. We have lately received your warning letters containing among other things that we should desist from the disturbances, grievances and troubles against the lord Gruffudd ap Gwenwynwyn and our brother David and should make due satisfaction and that we should observe the composition of agreement between us and the said lords completely in all and singular its articles without any diminution.

(Letter of Prince Llywelyn to the Bishops of Bangor and St Asaph, 20 December 1274. *Littere Wallie*, p.174.)

D.7   [Llywelyn] has been a vigorous and special protector of our Order and of all ecclesiastical Orders and persons in Wales in times of peace and in war. So we humbly beg you, Holy Father, on our knees, that, inspired by divine love, you will not believe such references as the bishop of St Asaph has made concerning the said prince.

(Letter to Pope Gregory X from the Abbots of Whitland, Strata Florida, Cwm-hir, Strata Marcella, Aberconwy, Cymer, Valle Crucis. A.W. Haddan and W. Stubbs, *Councils and Ecclesiastical Documents relating to Great Britain and Ireland*, I (3 vols.), Oxford, 1869–78, p.499.)

D.8   When, a short time ago, controversy broke out concerning the rights and liberties of the church of Asaph between Llywelyn, prince of Wales, on the one side, and Anian, bishop of that place, on the other, the same bishop, wishing to inquire more precisely from senior clerics and laymen, worthy of belief, who knew the truth concerning these matters, what the same rights had been and, by diligent examination, could bring them to light, . . . called together at St Asaph the *chapter* and other trustworthy clerics and laymen, who were excellently informed on these matters, instructed not through hearsay but by thorough personal knowledge of all these matters . . . they disclosed to him frequent complaints [against Llywelyn] and manifest injury [caused by him].

(19 October 1274. Diocesan Assembly at St Asaph respecting the liberties of the diocese. Haddan and Stubbs, *Councils*, I, pp.502–3.)

D.9   . . . We wish to make known to you, Holy Father, by these present letters that both our predecessors and we ourselves . . . have been in peaceful possession of those said liberties and customs which [Bishop Anian] claims. And if by charters of our predecessors granting the said liberties and customs to the church of Asaph they can be shown to belong to that church by law, we shall be prepared to concede them to the same church without contention. But if, however, we and our predecessors are lawfully in possession of those liberties and customs they shall be kept as before.

(25 May 1275. Prince Llywelyn to Robert Kilwardby, Archbishop of Canterbury. Haddan and Stubbs, *Councils*, I, pp.503–5.)

D.10   . . . on the king's recent withdrawal from the March, Llywelyn, prince of Wales, caused it to be published throughout his dominion that peace had been made between Llywelyn and the king, and that the king had withdrawn; and on this pretext, the prince had imposed on the people a heavy tribute of threepence on each head of cattle, and on other animals at his pleasure, which money he pretends he will pay to the king. Wherefore some people are astonished and afraid, and suggest to Anian that he should report the matter to the king.

(Soon after September 1275. Anian of St Asaph to Edward I. Edwards, *Calendar of Ancient Correspondence*, p.105.)

Illustration from the Anian Pontifical, Bangor. (*Source: Dean and Chapter of Bangor Cathedral.*)

D.11 ... we grant for ourselves and our heirs to the same bishop and his successors in the church of St Asaph that they should have and peacefully enjoy all those rights, liberties, possessions, and customs, which the same bishop and his predecessors in that place used and enjoyed since the time of our father of blessed memory, King Henry ...

(20 January 1276. Confirmation of the liberties of St Asaph by Edward I to Bishop Anian. Haddan and Stubbs, *Councils*, I, p.509.)

D.12 ... these liberties, rights, and customs which have been in the possession of the said church from time immemorial, that same prince, to the peril of his immortal soul and against justice, usurps and unlawfully detains; concerning which, the supreme pontiff, Gregory X, at the instance of the bishop and *chapter*, directed his letters, especially concerning certain articles of which it was clear that the church enjoyed possession, that he [Llywelyn] should desist from all occupation of them at once ...

(7 December 1276. Bishop and Chapter of St Asaph: declaration of grievances against Prince Llywelyn. Haddan and Stubbs, *Councils*, I, pp.511–16.)

D.13 That his serene Highness, the Lord Prince Edward, by the grace of God illustrious King of England, who has built in the vicinity a famous and fine place, newly defended with towers and ditches, wishes to move the see to that place [Rhuddlan]; and offers sufficient space and 1,000 marks for the building of a church. I therefore beg your Holiness to pay heed to the request of the king and allow him to make the translation; on condition that in your letters of approval you expressly mention that the liberties and customs of the church shall be conserved and approved when the translation or removal of the new place [takes effect].

(May or June 1281. Bishop Anian to Pope Martin IV. Haddan and Stubbs, *Councils*, I, p.529.)

D.14   Those who are jealous of the bishop have told the king that the bishop loves the Prince of Wales and his own people, and this is certainly true, provided that he can do it with a good conscience and saving the honour of God and the Church. But because the prince has offended God and the Church in many things, and has endeavoured to withdraw his *homage* from his liege lord the king, to the king's prejudice and in perturbation of the realm, the bishop has . . . publicly *excommunicated* the prince, though few in the realm could have believed this of the bishop. For he had been the prince's confessor, and although he could not stir a foot except under the prince's power, yet being anxious to avoid offence to God and the king he had, after the celebration of mass on Palm Sunday, escaped and come into England, for fear of death or at least of arrest.

(Anian, Bishop of Bangor, to Edward I. Not long after 21 March 1277. Edwards, *Calendar of Ancient Correspondence*, p.66.)

D.15   . . . he lost his brother, his sister's son, his cousin and kinsmen to the number of sixty, in the king's service, and Llywelyn greatly rejoices at this misfortune. His tongue cannot suffice to tell his losses, the burnings of churches and the plunderings of his property in this war.

(Anian, Bishop of Bangor, to Robert, Bishop of Bath and Wells, Chancellor. Probably 1277. Edwards, *Calendar of Ancient Correspondence*, p.112.)

D.16   Ac ena y gwnaethpwyd brat lliwelyn ene clochte en mangor y gan y wyr ef ehun.
    (And then the betrayal of Llywelyn was conspired in the belfry in Bangor by his own men.)

(1282. Jones, *Brut y Tywysogyon, Peniarth MS 20 Version*, p.228.)

D.17   Papal mandate to the bishop of St Davids to collect a yearly hundredth of all church revenues in Wales, for five years for the Holy Land, giving him full powers and faculties to carry out this order, and by preaching, *indulgences*, and dispensations to induce and incite, or by censures to compel, all men to assist in the crusade, any *papal indult* to the contrary notwithstanding.

(3 October 1263. Davies, *Episcopal Acts*, p.405.)

D.18 I [Bishop Thomas Bek] ordain and enact that in the town of Llawhaden, at a place specially appointed by me for the purpose where I have erected an *oratory*, shall be built a hospital in which pilgrims, orphan paupers, infirm, old and feeble persons and imbecile strangers, and wearied travellers may be entertained.

(November 1287. G. Hartwell Jones, 'Celtic Britain and the Pilgrim Movement', *Y Cymmrodor*, Vol.XXIII, 1912, p.450.)

D.19 . . . Cawr mawr bychan,
Cryf, cadarn, gwan, gwynion ruddiau;
Cyfoethog, tlawd,
A'n Tad a'n Brawd, awdur brodiau.
Iesu yw hwn
A erbyniwn yn ben rhiau.

(Madog ap Gwallter's 'Geni Crist'. Thomas Parry (ed.), *Oxford Book of Welsh Verse*, Oxford, 1962, pp.43–4.)

. . . Great giant small and frail,
So mighty yet so weak, with cheek how pale,
So rich, so poor is he,
Our Father-Brother and our Judge to be.
Jesus is he
Whom we receive as chief lord to be.)

(Madog ap Gwallter's 'Birth of Christ', H.I. Bell, *A History of Welsh Literature*, Oxford, 1955, p.56.)

D.20 . . . We pray that you will choose to preserve the pristine liberties and rights of the Church of Wales, so happily transferred to your rule, that the increase in your honour may not turn to the mourning of the Church . . . on that account we write to your Majesty that those new lords or *bailiffs*, to whom you have entrusted the government of Wales, carnally wise but spiritually foolish, so divide the liberty that everything which seems to them to accord with the laws of England they take full possession of; everything of benefit to the Church which differs from English custom they destroy and overturn.

> (3 July 1284. Archbishop Pecham to Edward I. Haddan and Stubbs, *Councils*, I, pp.569–70.)

D.21 First of all, sire, the savagery [of the Welsh] and other evils arise from this cause, that they do not live together but dwell far apart from each other. And so, sire, if you wish to make them behave in accordance with God and the world, and take away their savagery, command them to live in towns . . . Therefore, sire, the people will never learn virtue nor be well behaved except in so far as they have those who know how to teach them; and that cannot be unless they are compelled to send their children to England to acquire scholarship and manners; because the clerics of their country scarcely know the letters which they read.

> (8 July 1284. Pecham to Edward I. Translated from Old French. Haddan and Stubbs, *Councils*, I, pp.570–1.)

Debating the Evidence

Documents relating to religious matters and to ecclesiastical property rights form a high proportion of surviving medieval records. The clergy were, of course, the custodians of literacy and learning and this predisposed them to commit to writing matters which laymen might be less able to. Clergymen provided the clerical and administrative support that monarchs and *feudal* lords required to regularize their control of their subordinates, to secure their own rights and simply to record what was done and what was ordained. So we know a lot, relatively speaking, about Church life in the Middle Ages.

Source D.1
What does the form of this agreement tell us about the importance of the clergy in the secular life of medieval society?

Source D.2
What specific action did *Gerald* mean by describing the Welsh nation as being unjustly 'separated from the body of Christ'? *Gerald* can scarcely be called an objective witness, but his strong partialities are usually

obvious enough to be discerned as such, and sometimes he even contradicts his own prejudices. What is the especial value of such testimony compared to other forms of documentary evidence?

Source D.3
Why was the status of the Welsh dioceses in relation to Canterbury of great importance to the Crown as well as to the English primate? What does the phrase 'saving his order' mean, and what does it tell us about Bishop Richard?

Source D.4
Detailed studies of the Welsh chronicles since the 1940s have shown how *Brut y Tywysogyon* and the related *Annales Cambriae* developed out of Latin chronicles compiled at various monastic centres, including early material compiled at St Davids and Whitland. What internal evidence might be adduced in an attempt to establish where a chronicle or its component sections was compiled?

Source D.5
The phrase 'the form of peace' occurs in many of the letters from Llywelyn himself to Edward I after 1277. To what does it refer? William of Llanfaes had previously attended the King on Llywelyn's behalf concerning a long-running legal dispute over goods from a wreck. What special qualities might a cleric, and a friar in particular, bring to such negotiations?

Source D.6
Does Llywelyn's response suggest that the bishops were acting in an appropriate role as arbitrators? How would Llywelyn interpret the intercession of these two bishops in his dispute with Dafydd and Gruffudd ap Gwenwynwyn? A feature worthy of note is that 1274 had seen a plot by these two lords to assassinate Llywelyn.

Source D.7
Does this letter suggest anything about the Cistercian order as a body, notwithstanding the particular subject of the letter? A rich area for local research is the influence of monastic houses on the development of agricultural settlement and even urbanization in different parts of Wales, through their control of extensive farmland, parish churches, mills and

often complete medieval townships. The pattern of foundation and endowment can be studied in Professor Williams's *Welsh Church from Conquest to Reformation*, F.G. Cowley's *The Monastic Order in South Wales* and David H. Williams's *The Welsh Cistercians*. A mass of information is tabulated in Knowles and Hadcock's *Medieval Religious Houses*.

Sources D.8 and D.9
How far do these two documents shed light on how customary rights, both individual and corporate, were maintained in the Middle Ages? Compare this account with the well-documented process by which a massive compendium such as *Domesday Book* was prepared two centuries earlier. The limit of 'legal memory' was fixed at 1189 in Edward I's own legal reforms. The enormous disparity between the allegedly seventh to ninth-century donations of land recorded in the *Liber Landavensis* and the book's twelfth-century provenance presents the historian with a serious problem in evaluating even the sparse early medieval documentation that has survived. Why should such a large number of charters have survived the phenomenal loss-rate of medieval documents, especially in the form of later 'inspection' copies?

Source D.10
This document might be used as evidence of duplicity and oppressive exaction on the part of Llywelyn. What would be its weakness as evidence of such a case?

Source D.11
Many royal charters or grants were made to confirm rights or privileges granted previously. Can a rough timescale for the original grant which this document confirms be deduced from the document itself?

Source D.12
What unchallengeable sanction, in terms of legal process, does this document imply is at the author's disposal?

Source D.13
Why would such a move as Bishop Anian is describing here be advantageous to both king and bishop? What impression does the document convey of Bishop Anian's main concerns at the time?

Source D.14
What does Bishop Anian of Bangor's opening sentence indicate about the attitudes of people close to Edward I towards Llywelyn and the Welsh at this time? Would Anian's action be regarded as characteristic of him? On the face of it, might such an action have seemed more consistent with what we know of Anian of St Asaph?

Source D.15
How might Bishop Anian of St Asaph's attitude to Llywelyn be summed up from the body of evidence presented here? Is this acceptable as evidence of mutual antipathy? What does the document tell us of the scale and impact of the 1276–7 conflict between Llywelyn and the King?

Source D.16
This cryptic, famous, sentence stands alone as evidence of a conspiracy against Llywelyn among the Bangor clergy. Totally uncorroborated as it is, it cannot be taken as conclusive evidence of a plot. It can be used, however, as tentative evidence of something else. What might that be?

Source D.17
How might a thirteenth-century cleric proceed to carry out the Pope's mandate to promote the crusade? Why should it have been important to Christians so far from the Holy Land? What other evidence is there, within this period, that the 'moral imperative' of the crusade still had powerful lay support?

Source D.18
Thomas Bek was one of the 'builder bishops' of St Davids. He added to the Bishop's Palace at St Davids and strengthened the administration of the see. Despite the high spiritual tone of the ordinance quoted here, the township of Llawhaden could boast one building that showed the medieval Church at its most secular. What was this building? Did its presence make Llawhaden a sensible place to build a hospital?

Source D.19
Why were striking paradoxes such as those expressed in this poem central to the Christian view of Jesus? How did the Church itself, especially the monastic orders, seek to express these paradoxes?

Source D.20
Is there anything in this extract which might explain Bishop Anian of St Asaph's action against the English soldiery? How might the trends Archbishop Pecham is warning against here have affected future prospects for harmony within Wales?

Source D.21
Was Archbishop Pecham in a position in 1284 to judge the educational standards of the Welsh clergy? His comments on the lack of urban development in Wales echoed those of *Gerald of Wales* nearly a full century earlier. There were, however, communities called 'trefi' (townships) which had cohesive community organization, all over native Wales. Llywelyn ap Gruffudd had established some boroughs with clearly defined rights and privileges. Yet Wales was over-whelmingly perceived as a society without towns. What characteristics of the structure of Welsh free townships might explain this phenomenon?

Discussion

The sources in this section are more varied than for any other section in this volume. This is what we would expect. Clerics were the most important sources of written evidence in the Middle Ages, and they showed a versatility in writing about themselves and their activities that they rarely extended to others. So it is that these sources help us to penetrate rather further into the thought-world of medieval society than we are normally permitted to do. Most of the sources, it is true, are about the institutional life of the Church; but we are allowed glimpses also of men and women's religious convictions — notably of the cult of the human Jesus (D.19), of the charitable foundation of hospitals (D.18) and of the continuing appeal of the crusade, at least financially (D.17). Ecclesiastical documents, appropriately enough, also have an international dimension so often lacking in secular sources. Churchmen were, after all, members of an international order of clergy and owed their ultimate allegiance to Rome. This international flavour comes out strongly in the sources — in the appeal of the Welsh Cistercian abbots, themselves members of a self-consciously international movement, to the Pope (D.7) or in the way that a bishop of St Davids goes to Rome to be consecrated (D.3).

But, whether it liked it or not, the Church was of this world and the sources show vividly the nature of its ties with lay society. The Church was the United Nations peace-keeping force of the period. Our sources show it confirming a key agreement between two Welsh political leaders (D.1) and trying to keep them to the straight and narrow of those agreements (D.6). It also reminded rulers, even victorious ones like Edward I, of their general moral and spiritual responsibilities (D.20, D.21). We have to ask ourselves whether the Church was really as powerful as its own rhetoric suggested. Did its ecclesiastical penalties really make a difference? Do we overrate its power simply because it has left so much evidence about itself and its views? Thus Archbishop Pecham made some fascinating comments on the Welsh and their 'savagery' (D.21); but was his plan for the re-education and urbanization of the Welsh acted upon? Indeed, his letter might prompt you to think whether you learn more from it about Archbishop Pecham's view of what constituted 'civilization' than about the Welsh.

Two other features stand out from the sources. The one is the way the Church often seemed to be used by the king for his own ends, to excommunicate his enemies (D.14) and to support his policies (D.21). Do you get the impression from the sources that the Church's independence was compromised by its secular affiliations? Was this the point that *Gerald of Wales* was making (D.2) and does it have a contemporary resonance? Secondly, the sources in this section give the impression — and rightly so — that the Church was obsessed about its 'liberties and customs' (D.8, D.9, D.10, D.11). Those 'liberties' were what we would call privileges, and the Church defended them fiercely. Is it any wonder that it has been called the 'greatest closed shop there ever was'? Do the sources leave you with the impression that the Church was more concerned about those privileges than about the practice of religion? Or is that to let our sources distort our view?

Crown and Communities: Collaboration and Conflict

A.D. CARR

On 9 July 1283 six of the 'more noble, more honest and more trustworthy' men of each of the mainland *cantrefs* of Gwynedd, acting on behalf of their communities, entered into bonds before the Bishop of Bangor to maintain the peace (E.1). These undertakings, made shortly after the capture of the last native prince of Wales, Dafydd ap Gruffudd, really mark the end of the last war of Welsh independence; the Statute of Wales, issued at Rhuddlan eight months later, contained Edward I's new administrative and legal arrangements for the principality which had come into his possession. If political independence, as we understand the term, had come to an end, the principality of Wales, granted in 1301 to the King's eldest surviving son, Edward of Caernarfon, retained its autonomy; it did not become part of the kingdom of England.

The Statute superimposed a new pattern of counties on the existing system of *cantrefs* and *commotes*; in the south the counties of Cardigan and Carmarthen had been in existence since 1241, but in the north the counties of Anglesey, Caernarfon and Merioneth were new creations. The native princes' central administration was replaced by a royal governor, the Justice of North Wales; his counterpart in the two southern counties first appears in 1280. In effect, as was said in the answer to one of the petitions from the community of north Wales in 1305, the justice replaced the prince's *seneschal* or *distain* (E.2). Each county had a *sheriff*; of the sixteen men who held the office in north Wales during Edward's reign, five were Welsh. And in each *commote* the *rhaglaw* and the *rhingyll*, now representatives of the Crown as they had been of the prince before the conquest,

E.1

E.2

continued to be Welsh. Such men had always been drawn from those *kindreds* which were the leaders of their communities and the offices seem often to have been hereditary (E.3A). When Goronwy Crach, the *rhingyll* or beadle of the *commote* of Menai in Anglesey, complained to Edward of Caernarfon in 1305 that he was being forced to pay an annual rent for the office which he and his ancestors had held without payment, it was ruled that he could retain the office for three pounds annually but that he must relinquish all the rights which he and his heirs had in it (E.3B). This suggests that Edward realized, as many Anglo-Norman lords had long done, that at the local level Welshmen were best governed through their own leaders; however, the document also suggests that he was not prepared to recognize hereditary rights to offices which would deprive him and his successors of a valuable source of patronage. Welshmen could be the beneficiaries of such patronage, as was the royal servant from Anglesey, Tudur ap Gruffudd, granted the office of *rhaglaw* of the *commote* of Talybolion in his native county in recognition of his service to the king (E.4).

The medieval concept of the community is not easily defined. In the principality it could mean the Welsh or the English immigrants who lived mainly in the new boroughs. And an individual could belong simultaneously to several communities; he stood at the centre of a series of concentric circles, representing his own neighbourhood, the county and the principality. The community was essentially the people, rather than the territorial administrative unit, and the term was also applied to the leaders of those people, who spoke for them and acted on their behalf. The county court, introduced by Edward in the Statute of Wales, provided these leaders with a forum where the king's wishes could be made known to them and where the royal representatives could negotiate over such matters as taxation and the maintenance of order; at the same time the community could make its grievances and requests known to the authorities.

As the principality of Wales was not part of the kingdom of England it was not represented in Parliament, nor was it subject to parliamentary taxation. Usually the authorities negotiated the payment of a *subsidy* with the representatives of the community, but on the first occasion when Wales was taxed in 1291, the *subsidy* granted to Edward to pay the ransom of his kinsman, the King of Sicily, was demanded from both the principality and the March (E.5). The *Marcher lords* were assured that it would not be regarded as a precedent and it was eventually paid (E.6). Madog ab Iorwerth, named in the *subsidy* roll entry for the township of Pennant-lliw in Merioneth, was typical of the men who represented the community; he held various offices in the county and the sum for which he was assessed must reflect his standing. Only three in Merioneth were assessed at a higher figure. But, despite the assurances to the *Marcher lords* in 1291, the royal lands in Wales were not to be free of the burden of taxation. A further *subsidy* was demanded in 1300, although Edward's conciliatory and tactful approach to the Welsh community is to be seen in the way in which it was reminded of its agreement (E.7A). And now this community was assured that payment was in no way to be considered a precedent (E.7B).

E.5
E.6

E.7A

E.7B

One consequence of the extension of English criminal law and procedure to the principality of Wales was the laying of responsibility for the maintenance of order on the community. At some time in Edward's reign, probably not long after the revolt of Madog ap Llywelyn (see below), the justice met the community of each county and a series of ordinances providing for the maintenance of order was drawn up (E.8). Some of these ordinances extended English practice to the principality; others may have been a restatement of pre-conquest practice. This new obligation of communal responsibility replaced the Welsh *ceisiad*, or sergeant of the peace, who had been sustained by a *food render* which seems to have been much resented; the community may well have welcomed the change.

E.8

For most people the new regime meant little change and the traditional leaders of the community retained their power and influence. Indeed, in some ways Gwynedd may have been better off under Edward than it had been under Llywelyn ap Gruffudd, whose heavy financial demands must have been a strain on his people's loyalty. Even so, there were two revolts in Wales between 1282 and Edward's death in 1307. The first, in Carmarthenshire in 1287, was led by *Rhys ap Maredudd*, a

E.9   member of the royal house of Deheubarth (E.9). Like most of the Welsh lords outside Gwynedd, Rhys had supported Edward in the war of 1276–7; unlike them, he had also taken his side in 1282. As a result he had expected to be better rewarded than he was; he had assumed that he would be the independent lord of Cantref Mawr, but he felt that he was being subjected to increasing pressure and interference from the Justice of South Wales. In June 1287 he rebelled, but by January 1288 the revolt had been suppressed by a royal army which included a large Welsh contingent. Rhys was eventually captured and executed at York.

     This revolt cannot in any way be seen as a national rising or as a protest by the Welsh community against misgovernment; it was the reaction of a disappointed and frustrated Welsh lord. The second revolt, which broke out in September 1294, was far

E.10   more serious and affected the whole of Wales (E.10). The leader in the north was Madog ap Llywelyn, one of the sons of the last lord of Meirionnydd who had been ejected by Llywelyn ap Gruffudd in 1256. He had already tried unsuccessfully to recover his inheritance, as had Morgan ap Maredudd of Gwynllwg, the leader of the Glamorgan rebels; the revolt in the south west was led by Maelgwn ap Rhys, a descendant of the house of Deheubarth. At first the rebels had the advantage of surprise, but by the early summer of 1295 the revolt was over, having been put down by a major military campaign. On the face of it, the revolt was a co-ordinated protest by members of the native aristocracy. But there was more to it than that. It can be seen, particularly in north Wales, as a protest by the community. It is hardly likely that there was much sympathy for the grievances of Madog himself and unlikely, too, that there was much sentiment at the time for the return of the native dynasty of which he was a cadet.

     A combination of causes may have driven the community to rebel. Llywelyn's last years had been a time of abnormal financial pressures on the Gwynedd community. When Edward's officials surveyed his new territories after the conquest it is possible that they assumed that the payments and services exacted from the community in the years immediately preceding the Prince's death were the normal pattern. This was

reflected in the *Extents* made after the conquest, which were to
lead to a good deal of protest (E.11). The *bondmen* of the *demesne*
township of Penrhosllugwy in Anglesey complained again in
1315, 1322 and 1327; each time they proved their point but for a
long time the authorities went on trying to collect the extra
money. In addition to these excessive demands, the *subsidy* of
1291 was levied in Wales as well as in England and in 1294 an
attempt was made to conscript Welsh troops for the King's
campaign in Gascony. All this may have driven the community
to the limit and the participation of its leaders in the revolt may
have been an indication that Edward's officials had gone too far.

It is to Edward's credit that his subsequent response suggests
that he was aware of this. Although the revolt had caused him to
abandon a projected campaign in Gascony and although the
cost of putting it down was to lead to a major financial and
constitutional crisis in England, he seems to have realized that
something was radically wrong in the principality. Not long
after the revolt was finally suppressed, John de Havering,
the newly-appointed Justice of North Wales, and William
Sycun, the constable of Conwy Castle, were commissioned to
investigate the complaints of the community of north Wales
about maladministration by royal officials since the conquest
and to remedy them (E.12). The King certainly seems to have
been careful and considerate of Welsh feelings. In 1296 it was
brought to his attention by a deputation representing the
community, made up of three Welshmen and the English *sheriff*
of Anglesey, that there was a rumour in north Wales that he was
suspicious of them. His response was a letter of reassurance
(E.13); at the same time he wrote to the Justice instructing him
to deal severely with anyone spreading such rumours 'that the
punishment shall strike terror into others saying the like things'.
This tactful and conciliatory attitude may have been inspired by
fear of another revolt but it seems to have evoked a response, at
least for the rest of Edward's reign. And although Madog ap
Llywelyn himself was imprisoned, he was not executed and his
lands in Anglesey were inherited by one of his sons.

When the principality was granted to Edward of Caernarfon
in 1301, the new prince came to Wales to receive the *homage* and
fealty of his subjects and all the leading members of the

E.11

E.12

E.13

E.14

community attended in their turn to accept him as their ruler (E.14). Sir Gruffydd Llwyd, who headed this part of the list, was typical of these leaders. He was one of the descendants of *Llywelyn ab Iorwerth*'s *seneschal*, Ednyfed Fychan, and thus a member of the dominant *kindred* in north Wales. During the principate of Edward of Caernarfon he was to serve successively as *sheriff* of Caernarfonshire and Anglesey and, after the Prince ascended the throne as Edward II, he had two terms of office as *sheriff* of Merioneth. He seems to have been regarded as the leader of the Welsh of north Wales and for most of his life his loyalty to the Crown was conspicuous; he led the men of north Wales in the civil war of 1322 and he remained loyal to Edward II in the final crisis of his reign in 1326–7. Only once was his allegiance called in question; this was in the years after 1315 when *Robert Bruce* and his brother Edward had invaded Ireland and were planning an invasion of Wales. There is evidence that Sir Gruffydd was in contact with them and he seems to have been imprisoned for a time. But on the whole he represented the community which Edward handled with such care and which accepted the new order which left them in effective control at the local level.

Madog's revolt shows that the loyalty of the community was not to be taken for granted. Both the community and individuals were very ready to express their grievances. In 1305 a body of petitions from north Wales was submitted to Edward of Caernarfon at his manor of Kennington in Surrey. Of these petitions, 32 came from the community. Some reflect the tension which was already developing between the people of the principality and the new English boroughs established by Edward as part of his settlement. The community resented being compelled to trade in the boroughs, while the *burgesses* complained on several occasions that people were not coming to their markets and fairs to trade and that they were therefore losing the income from their tolls (E.15, E.16). This tension was to become worse during the fourteenth century.

E.15
E.16

One of the main communal grievances was to do with the right to buy and sell land. The Statute of Wales provided that the tenure of land should continue to be governed by Welsh law; this meant that free hereditary land was vested in the *kindred* and that no individual could sell his inheritance. In 1305 the community asked for the right to buy and sell land; they were told that the Prince was not prepared to make any change (E.17). This was not the end of the matter; at the Lincoln Parliament of 1316 they were given the right to buy and sell land for a period of three years (E.18). At the time Edward II was particularly anxious to be conciliatory, especially in view of the threat from the Bruce brothers in Ireland and the recent revolt of *Llywelyn Bren* in Glamorgan. In 1321 the right was extended for a further four years but there is no evidence of any later renewal. The reference in the petition to a four-year term is presumably to the legal device of *prid* which made it possible to convey land under Welsh law. But the response to this petition shows that the community, however conservative it may have been in some respects, was demanding more change than the authorities were prepared to concede. As far as land was concerned, the new settlement was particularly conservative; the statute laid down that there was to be no change in the rule of partible succession (E.19). There were, however, ways in which division could be avoided and an undivided inheritance passed on to the eldest son (E.20).

E.17

E.18

E.19

E.20

In addition to the petitions submitted at Kennington by the community, there was a far greater number from individuals. Many of these had to do with offices, rights or privileges granted before the conquest, with which the officials of the principality were now attempting to interfere (E.21). Nor were these the only petitions; indeed, petition was the usual way by which members of the community approached the king or the prince and many have survived in addition to those of 1305 (E.22). These, too, often illustrate the reaction of the community to the new order.

E.21

E.22

The conquest and the Edwardian settlement brought both collaboration and conflict between the Crown and communities in Wales. The leaders of the communities in Gwynedd accepted and supported the new regime which left them in control of those communities, while the Crown in turn depended on them. They continued to hold the offices of *rhaglaw* and *rhingyll*, although now in the name of King Edward, rather than Prince Llywelyn; the King needed their goodwill and co-operation, although this was not to be taken for granted and the revolt of Madog ap Llywelyn showed that they were not to be pushed too far. Office, order and taxation show the extent of collaboration; Madog's revolt shows the possibility of conflict and the volume of petitions, both communal and individual, shows a readiness to complain and to draw attention to grievances. The response to these petitions shows a readiness on the part of the Crown to remedy these grievances or, at least to investigate them and, above all, to listen. This is particularly evident after the revolt which seems, for Edward I, to have been the moment of truth in his dealings with the Welsh of the principality. There were long-standing grievances, but on the whole Crown and communities collaborated and the King saw the one major conflict of the period as a warning. Whatever undercurrents of hostility or nostalgia there may have been, they did not manifest themselves for the remainder of Edward's reign.

standing grievances, but on the whole Crown and communities collaborated and the King saw the one major conflict of the period as a warning. Whatever undercurrents of hostility or nostalgia there may have been, they did not manifest themselves for the remainder of Edward's reign.

Sources

E.1   In the year of Our Lord one thousand two hundred and eighty three, on St Cyril's day, the community of the men of the *cantref* of Llyn being assembled at Llanerfyl before the lord Anian, by divine mercy bishop of Bangor, [it was agreed] by the unanimous and express consent of the aforesaid community, in order that the firm, faithful, stable and secure peace of the lord king and his kingdom should be maintained in the future, [that] six of the more honest, noble and trustworthy men from the aforesaid *cantref*, whose names are represented by the affixing of their seals [and] by whom the aforesaid peace may be more securely maintained, should by these presents bind themselves to the lord king or his heirs for the payment of two thousand

Harlech Castle. (*Source: Cadw: Welsh Historic Monuments Crown Copyright.*)

pounds by way of security for the faithful observance of the said peace . . .

(Bond of 9 July 1283. J.G. Edwards (ed.), *Littere Wallie*, preserved in Liber A in the Public Record Office, 1940, pp. 154–5.)

E.2 . . . It was answered that if anything was taken from anyone against his will by anyone, unless by order of the lord prince or his justice to the use of the prince's castles or towns or for the upkeep of the household of the prince or his justice, who is in the place of the *distain*, for the prices accustomed in the times of the king and the prince, for which he should satisfy them in due form, the takers should be severely punished before the justice on the complaint of the plaintiff . . .

(Kennington petitions, 1305. H. Ellis (ed.), *Registrum vulgariter nuncupatum. The Record of Caernarvon*, London, 1838, p.215.)

E.3A To the petition of Goronwy Crach that, whereas he and his ancestors in the time of the king and the prince held the office of *rhingyll* of the *commote* of Menai quit of any rent rendered for it, Sir Hugh de Leominster, keeper of the lady Queen of England, the mother of the prince, in the aforesaid *commote*, burdened the said ringildry with 60s . . .

E.3B Tudur son of Gruffydd of Anglesey, the king's servant who served him faithfully in Wales and Ireland, begs the king that he be given the *bailiwick* for the term of his life, rendering thence annually 60s. as long as he should bear himself well and faithfully towards the lord and that the arrears which were demanded from him by the justice for the farm of the aforesaid *bailiwick* from the time shown be repaid to him by the aforesaid council up to the feast of St Michael next ensuing. And for this grant the aforesaid Goronwy released and *quitclaimed* for himself and his heirs for ever to the said prince and his heirs all the right and claim which he had, or in any way could have in the office of the aforesaid ringildry and then he made his letters of *quitclaim* which remain in the custody of the prince's *chancery*.

(Kennington petitions, 1305. Ellis, *Record of Caernarvon*, p.219.)

E.4   Tudur son of Gruffydd of Anglesey, the king's servant who served him faithfully in Wales and Ireland, begs the king that the *bailiwick* of the *commote* of Talybolion in Anglesey, which the king granted him freely of his grace by his letters on account of his service in the war in which lord Llywelyn was killed and again granted to him after the last war in Wales by other letters of his, he will cause to be freely granted to him, because Hugh, the king's treasurer of Caernarfon, seeks money for the *bailiwick*, notwithstanding the grant in manner aforesaid.

> (*c.*1295–1302. William Rees (ed.), *Calendar of Ancient Petitions relating to Wales*, Cardiff, 1975, p.454–5.)

E.5   Request to the earls, barons, knights, free men and whole community of Wales to grant, in such manner as Richard de Massy and Master Adam de Bodindon, whom the king is sending to them shall more fully request a fifteenth like the rest of the realm, in order to pay the debts which the king incurred during his absence abroad in effecting the liberation of Charles, king of Sicily, his kinsman, whereby the state of the Holy Land and of the church was improved and peace secured; and to reply by the said messengers as to what they will do for the king.

> (20 January 1291. *Calendar of the Patent Rolls, 1292–1301*, London, 1895, p.419.)

E.6   Pennant-lliw
        Madog ab Iorwerth 30*s.*
        Einion Llwyd 13$\frac{1}{4}$*d.*
        Madog ab Einion 2*s.* 4*d.*
        Gruffydd Ddu 5*s* 2$\frac{3}{4}$*d.*
        Iorwerth ab Einion 2*s* 2$\frac{1}{2}$*d.*
        Iorwerth ap Gwahalet 3*s.* 8$\frac{1}{2}$*d.*
        Einion ap Gwahalet 16$\frac{3}{4}$*d* . . .

> (Keith Williams-Jones (ed.), *The Merioneth Lay Subsidy Roll 1292–3*, Cardiff, 1976, pp. 7–8.)

E.7A   Request to the good men and community of north Wales, in consideration of the king's indigence and of his being with his army in Scotland, to be good enough to pay the *subsidy* they have granted of their own good will for the Scotch war, and for which the king renders many thanks, to the said Master Richard, at a day and place which he will let them know, and they will not omit to do so, as they love the king's honour and advantage.

E.7B   Grant that the subvention of money in aid of the Scotch war, which the bishops, abbots, priors and whole community of north Wales of their good will have made to the king, shall not be to their prejudice or drawn into a precedent.

(10 July, 21 September 1300. *Calendar of the Patent Rolls, 1292–1301*, pp. 526, 534.)

E.8   . . . for the maintaining of the peace the justice caused to come before him all the more prominent and more honest Welshmen of the county, having full authority on behalf of the community of the whole county to ordain and decide, along with the counsel of the said justice, on a suitable remedy for the above-mentioned matters: which same more honest men, by an ordinance made between the justice and themselves, undertook for themselves and the whole community of the county to maintain the peace of the lord king in the same county.

(Ordinances, *c.*1296. Ellis, *Record of Caernarvon*, p.132.)

E.9   1287. *Rhys ap Maredudd*, lord of Ystrad Tywi, moved by a dispute between himself and Sir Robert Tibetot, then the lord king's justice of Carmarthen, on Sunday next before the feast of the blessed apostle Barnabas took the castles of Llandovery, Dinefwr and Carreg Cennen and afterwards burned the town of Swansea and the manor of Ystlwyf with the greater part of the land and town of Llanbadarn Fawr and the town of Carmarthen as far as the gates . . .

(1287. J. Williams ab Ithel (ed.), *Annales Cambriae*, London, 1860, p.109.)

E.10   In the same year, around the feast of St Michael, the Welsh rose in rebellion. For they had met together and decided among themselves that on the same day of St Michael they would all rise together against the king and attack his castles, and thus they did and on the same day, as if by surprise, they took many castles and they took the castle of Caernarfon, which our king had not long since constructed at great expense, demolishing the walls and slaughtering the king's ministers, and those Englishmen who could, fled and many were overwhelmed with the edge of the sword ... Moreover, the instigators of this treason were two named Madog and Morgan, who said that they were descended from the stock of Prince Llywelyn and that they should therefore assume the name of prince.

(1294. H. Rothwell (ed.), *The Chronicle of Walter of Guisborough*, Royal Historical Society, Camden Third Series, LXXXIX, London, 1957, p.251.)

E.11   To the petition to the prince of the *villeins* of the *maerdref* of Penrhos that the *sheriff* compelled them to pay £24 annually of an unjust extent. And to the petition of the prince's *villeins* of Rhosyr that the justice distrained them to pay 12s. 9d. of annual rent of assize of an unjust extent in addition to what they were accustomed to pay. It was answered that what was put in the extent made in the time of the king before the land of Wales was given to the lord prince could not be remitted unless they showed a charter or title, but the justice was then instructed to have the extent examined and if an error should be found in it he should certify the lord of the error and meanwhile the demand should be respited.

(Kennington petitions, 1305. Ellis, *Record of Caernarvon*, p.217.)

E.12   The king to his beloved and faithful John de Havering, his justice of north Wales, and William Sycun, constable of his castle of Aberconwy, greeting. Because we have learned from the serious complaint of the men of the community of north Wales that the *sheriffs*, *bailiffs* and all our ministers of those parts have inflicted various trespasses, injuries, extortions, oppressions and grievous losses on the same men from the time that those lands came into our hands and that they still do not refrain from inflicting [them] from day to day, to the grave loss and manifest impoverishment of the men of the same community, we, therefore, wishing that justice should be brought to the aid of the same men, have appointed you our justices in this matter to enquire by the oath of honest and law-worthy men of those parts . . . and then to do them justice according to the law and custom of those parts.

(Patent Rolls, 1 September 1295. J.E. Morris, *The Welsh Wars of King Edward the First: a Contribution to Medieval Military History*, Oxford University Press, 1901, p.266.)

E.13   Letter to the good men and community of Snowdon and Anglesey, informing them that the abbot of Aberconwy, Thomas Danvers, Tudur ap Goronwy and Hywel ap Cynwrig, sent by them to the king's presence, have related to the king the rumour which disturbed and grieved them, to wit, that the king held them in suspicion; and begging them not to believe such rumours for the future, as no sinister rumours of their state or behaviour has reached the king in these days and he has no suspicion towards them, but rather, by reason of their late good service, holds them for his faithful and devoted subjects.

(3 December 1296. *Calendar of the Patent Rolls, 1292–1301*, p.223.)

E.14   The 22nd day of April [of the 19th year] at the castle of Flint the underwritten men did *homage* and *fealty* to the lord Edward, son of Edward:
Sir Gruffydd Llwyd, knight
Tudur ap Goronwy of Anglesey
Madog ap Cynwrig, archdeacon of Anglesey and
Ieuan ap Hywel of Caernarfon
Tudur ap Gruffydd of Anglesey
Llywelyn ab Ednyfed of Anglesey
Gruffydd Fychan, son of Gruffydd ab Iorwerth of Anglesey
Madog Fychan of Englefield.

(22 April 1301. Edward Owen, *A list of those who did homage and fealty to the first English Prince of Wales, AD 1301*, privately printed, 1901, pp.3–4.)

E.15 To the common petition that individuals may buy and sell victuals, horses, oxen and cows for their own sustenances anywhere in the land outside markets and fairs so that they should not be threatened with prosecution or *amerced* for such buying and selling . . . It was answered that they should buy and sell in fairs and markets and nowhere else, except for small items of food like cheese, butter and milk changing hands for their own consumption far from markets . . .

(Kennington petitions, 1305. Ellis, *Record of Caernarvon*, p.212.)

E.16 And to the petition of the same *burgesses* [of Beaumaris] that although the lord prince ordained that the three *commotes* nearest the aforesaid town should all come to the market of Beaumaris with all their merchandise, all the men of the aforesaid *commotes* have withdrawn themselves from the aforesaid town and go to the town of Newborough and display their merchandise for sale there because the *burgesses* there are all Welsh. It was answered that the justice was ordered that he should enforce the ordinance.

(Kennington petitions, 1305. Ellis, *Record of Caernarvon*, p.223.)

E.17 To the common petition of the Welsh of north Wales that they should be able to buy and sell lands in Wales: this would be a change in the law of those parts since none of them could sell land or let it for a term, except for a term of four years. And although they say that the king granted this article, it does not appear to the prince nor to his council that it was granted to them by the king, since those things granted to them by the king are expressly contained in his grant made to them, namely in the Statute of Rhuddlan, in which no mention was made of that article, nor does the prince intend to change the law in this case [which was] by decree of the king himself, because the king handed that land over to him to hold to himself and his heirs of the kings of England.

(Kennington petitions, 1305. Ellis, *Record of Caernarvon*, p.214.)

E.18 . . . And that the freemen of Wales may be able for three years immediately following to sell and give lands, tenements and their rents to other free Welshmen . . .

(Lincoln Ordinances, 1316. Ivor Bowen, *The Statutes of Wales*, London, 1908, p.29.)

E.19   Whereas the custom is otherwise in Wales than in England concerning succession to an inheritance, inasmuch as the inheritance is *partible* among the heirs male, and from time whereof the memory of man is not to the contrary hath been *partible*, our lord the king will not have that custom abrogated; but willeth that inheritances shall remain *partible* among like heirs as it was wont to be; and partition of the same inheritances shall be made as it was wont to be made . . .

(Statute of Wales, 1284. Bowen, *The Statutes of Wales*, pp.25–6.)

E.20   Richard de Puleston, in consideration of service to the king's father and mother, prays the king that, as he holds of him 30 of land in Wales by *Welshry*, by which after his days the land would be *partible* between his ten sons and none of them could be maintained from his part, the king will take the land into his hand and after fifteen days make estate of it to Richard and Agnes his wife for life and afterwards to each one of his sons and the heirs male of their bodies, with reversion to Richard and his heirs, doing to the king the service of the twelfth part of a *knight's fee.*

(2 July 1309. *Calendar of Chancery Warrants, 1244–1326*, London, 1927, p.289.)

E.21   To the petition of Dafydd Fychan ap Dafydd ap Gwion, free tenant of the *cantref* of Llyn, that he may erect a mill in the place where his father and his ancestors had a mill in the times of the princes of Wales, of which the justice of north Wales and the *sheriff* of Caernarfon unjustly disturbed him. It was answered that the justice would find out if a mill had been there in the past and that if he held it by inheritance it would be allowed.

(Kennington petitions, 1305. Ellis, *Record of Caernarvon*, p.216.)

E.22   The community of the free men of all Anglesey show to the king that they are aggrieved, as it seems to them, in the underwritten articles: firstly, that they are compelled to make suit at the king's mill otherwise than they did in the time of the prince of Wales.

Secondly, that the foreign tenants of the free men are compelled to the king's *avowry*, which they never did in the time of the prince of Wales.

Thirdly, that those holding less than a *carucate* of land, or thereabouts, are distrained to do suit at the County Court, which heretofore they have not been compelled to do in the king's time; whence they seek that the king will release them and remove these burdens from them.

The descendants of Iorwerth ap Llywarch of the *commote* of Menai in Anglesey seek that they may have their ferry at Llanidan in the same *commote* as they were wont to have in the time of all the princes, freely and quietly, until Hugh de Leominster compelled them to pay 20*s.* yearly for the eight years now last past, although they paid nothing before to any prince or to the existing king.

(*c.*1300. Rees, *Calendar of Ancient Petitions relating to Wales*, p.452.)

Debating the Evidence

One of the most difficult things about writing the history of a conquered people is obtaining contemporary evidence of how the conquered reacted and adapted. The most ruthless conquests seem to wage war on future history as much as on immediate foes, by seeking to expunge every trace of the past of those they have vanquished as well as their present. The Edwardian conquest of Wales certainly did not fall into this category. A great deal of documentation survives which shows how Welsh communities coped with the reality of conquest, and there is strong evidence of the Crown's own desire to ameliorate the harsher abuses to which the defeated might be subject. How much of the Crown's concern was manifested in action at the local level is, of course, another matter.

Source E.1
The famous American phrase 'the consent of the governed' is clearly anachronistic in a medieval context, but what phrases in this extract might be used to argue that local consultation was important? With regard to what aspect of government does the document suggest that local support was important? How was the community 'encouraged' to ensure that collaboration worked?

Source E.2
Modern terminology, which carries built-in assumptions drawn from today's circumstances, cannot always describe medieval practice correctly. Notwithstanding this constraint, some analogies may be drawn as discussion aids. Which of the following modern terms, for example, might be most appropriate to describe the powers reserved in Source E.2 for the Prince's justice?
a) commandeering
b) requisitioning
c) compulsory purchase

Sources E.3A and E.3B
What do these documents suggest about the concerns of the royal chanceries and their clerks? What effects will such concerns have had upon the body of evidence these *chancery* documents can provide today? Can the process by which justice was done at the Prince's manor of Kennington be visualized or described on the basis of these documents?

Source E.4
How could this document be used to show the importance of the right to petition the king himself, from the viewpoints of both king and subject? Would there be pitfalls in using this document as evidence of a general, cumulative disaffection among the Welsh with certain aspects of the Edwardian regime?

Sources E.5, E.7A, E.7B
Does the tone of these documents convey anything about the King's approach to securing *subsidies* from the principality?

Source E.6
Of what use can a document such as the Lay *Subsidy* Roll be to the local

historian? What additional sources of information would enhance its value?

Source E.8
Does this extract suggest that the Welsh of the new shire of Caernarfon put forward their own representatives to frame law-enforcement ordinances with the justice's counsel?

Source E.9
Why should *Rhys ap Maredudd* have felt particularly aggrieved at his treatment at the hands of the justice of Carmarthen?

Source E.10
What evidence of co-ordination does the chronicler present in this account of Madog's rebellion? Does the account imply anything of Caernarfon's administrative importance under Edward I?

Source E.11
Why should the officials of the principality have attached so much importance to the *Extents* made in the 1280s and 1290s? Dr Carr has proposed that the payments recorded in the *Extents* reflected an abnormally high level of exaction deriving from Llywelyn's last years. Does the Prince's reply to these petitions display a willingness to recognize that such might be the case?

Source E.12
What flaw might be detected in Edward's proposed remedy for the catalogue of abuses recorded in this document?

Source E.13
A number of sources from this period express generalized opinions about the Welsh, often derogatory. Even Archbishop Pecham once called the Welsh 'a race of adulterers'. Edward I himself had summoned the Parliament of 1283 with this observation: 'The tongue of man can scarcely recount in detail the range of deceptions and plots which the Welsh race, with the stealth of foxes and with utter lack of respect for God and man, has committed against our predecessors and against our kingdom from time immemorial . . .' What does this document reveal about the day-to-day level of communication between the Crown and

the Welsh community in the 1290s? What circumstances made the Welsh especially sensitive to rumour? How might a rumour such as that mentioned in this extract have been spread?

Source E.14
What might the historian adduce from the association of these eight individuals in acts of *homage* and *fealty* on a single occasion?

Source E.15
Why should the Crown be reluctant to ease the ban on trading outside the royal boroughs? Might any reason other than loss of revenue incline the Crown to take this view?

Source E.16
What does this document, together with Source E.15, reveal about the role of the castle boroughs in the King's Welsh policy?

Sources E.17, E.18, E.19
How might it be possible to argue that these three documents illustrate:
a) the Crown's position as fountainhead of authority in making and unmaking law;
b) the role of the Crown as the prime judicial arbiter or interpreter of customary law;
c) an overriding concern to maintain customary practice and usage, while being prepared to make occasional and individual exceptions?

Source E.20
Does this document betray any hint of an assumption that inheritance by primogeniture is more desirable than *partible inheritance*, or a subjective judgement upon the economic effects of one compared with the other?

Sources E.21 and E.22
What criterion of legal validity is advocated in respect of proprietary rights and customary obligations by complainants in these extracts? Comparing Source E.22 with Source A.14 in the section on 'Welsh Society and Native Rule before the Conquest', can any shift of opinion be discerned over the intervening years? What qualifications would need to apply to any conclusions drawn from this comparison?

Discussion

After the Edwardian Conquest the Welsh historian enters what is for him the documentary clover. The reasons are twofold. Most of the written documents of pre-conquest Wales — and we have no clue how many there were — were probably destroyed at the conquest. That makes the contrast between pre- and post-conquest Wales appear sharper in written evidence than it probably was in reality. Secondly, the new English government was almost obsessively document-minded. Keeping records was one way of keeping control — and of ensuring that no rights and dues were overlooked through a lapse of memory. Note, for example, how the government kept a record of who submitted to it and on what terms (E.1), who owed tax and how much (E.6) and who had done homage (E.14). Collecting and processing such information could not have been easy. There were immense language problems to be overcome: how could a monoglot Welsh peasant communicate with an English sheriff and would the sheriff or his clerk understand some of the Welsh customs, names and dues? You need to bear that limitation in mind; you need also to remember that certain set formulae were used. Who, for example, were 'the more prominent and more honest' men referred to in E.8?

The most significant kind of source quoted in this section is the petition; there are twelve petitions, overwhelmingly from those submitted to Edward of Caernarfon at his palace in Kennington in 1305 (E.2–E.4, E.11, E.15–E.17, E.21, E.22). They are an invaluable source for the historian, for they lay bare the anxieties and complaints of the governed and do so in great detail. They tell us a great deal about the past as well as the present (see especially E.21, E.22); they also show us tensions coming to the boil, as the English burgesses of Beaumaris tried to protect their privileges and the Welshmen of Anglesey tried equally hard to circumvent them (E.15, E.16). But petitions must be treated warily. They are full of tall stories, of men trying to win favours by stretching the truth to their advantage. Perhaps the most interesting are the communal petitions, the ones which talk of general grievances (E.17, E.22), since they articulate the complaints of a group rather than a private grudge. Who commissioned such general petitions, drafted them and paid for them? There must, presumably, have been some degree of concerted action and leadership, probably from those 'more prominent and more honest men' (E.8), the kind who had pledged themselves on behalf of the community in 1283 (E.1). Fascinating as petitions are, it is well to remember they will not tell us of the dreams and visions which lay behind the great revolt of 1294–5 (E.10) nor of the deep suspicions of their loyalty which clearly worried the men of Gwynedd after that revolt (E.13). Even when the documentation is relatively rich, as it is for Wales after 1284, the historian still has the difficult task of weighing it, assessing its reliability, deciding how to balance one genre of documentation (for example, petitions) against another and then constructing as credible and convincing a description and analysis as he can.

Further Reading

J. Beverley Smith, *Llywelyn ap Gruffudd: Tywysog Cymru*, Caerdydd, 1986.

Llinos Beverley Smith, 'Llywelyn ap Gruffydd and the Welsh Historical Consciousness' in *Welsh History Review*, 12, 1984–5.

A.D. Carr, *Llywelyn ap Gruffydd*, Cardiff, 1982.

S.B. Chrimes, *King Edward I's Policy in Wales*, Cardiff, 1969.

F.G. Cowley, *The Monastic Order in South Wales, 1066–1349*, Cardiff, 1977.

R.R. Davies, *Conquest, Coexistence and Change. Wales 1063–1415*, Oxford/Cardiff, 1987.

R.R. Davies, 'Law and National Identity in Thirteenth-Century Wales' in *Welsh Society and Nationhood*, ed. R.R. Davies and others, Cardiff, 1984.

R.R. Davies, *Lordship and Society in the March of Wales 1282–1400*, Oxford, 1978.

R. Ian Jack, *Medieval Wales* (Sources of History Series), London, 1972.

J.E. Lloyd, *A History of Wales from the Earliest Times to the Edwardian Conquest*, 3rd edition, London, 1939.

F.M. Powicke, *King Henry III and the Lord Edward*, Oxford, 1947.

William Rees, *An Historical Atlas of Wales from Early Modern Times*, 2nd edition, London, 1959.

Glyn Roberts, *Aspects of Welsh History*, Cardiff, 1969.

D. Stephenson, *The Governance of Gwynedd*, Cardiff, 1984.

A.J. Taylor, *The History of the King's Works in Wales 1277–1330*, London, 1973.

W.H. Waters, *The Edwardian Settlement of Wales in its Administrative and Legal Aspects*, Cardiff, 1935.

Glanmor Williams, *The Welsh Church from Conquest to Reformation*, 2nd edition, Cardiff, 1976.

Glossary

Absolution	Formal remission of penance by the Church, a recognition of forgiveness.
Advowson	The right of presentment, or of appointment to clerical livings.
Amerce	To levy a fine in a court of law.
Assizes	Sittings of legislative bodies and their decrees.
Augustinian Canons	Religious order developed in the eleventh century; followers of 'the rule of St Augustine'. Regular canons, as opposed to monks who lived the monastic life for its own sake, were essentially secular clergy attached to a church who chose, in addition, to live according to the monastic rule.
Avowry	Patronage and right of presentation to a benefice.
Bailiff	The agent or steward of the lord, prince or king in a particular district, or *bailiwick*.
Bailiwick	A district under a bailiff's jurisdiction.
Barons' Wars	The confrontation between *Simon de Montfort* and his followers and Henry III.
Bastide	A fortified and walled borough.
Benedictines	Monks following the rule of St Benedict, who established the order in the sixth century. The rule of Benedict was the basis of a number of monastic orders founded in the tenth century, the first being that of

Cluny (910) but the most important of which was that of the Cistercians, who wanted to return to the letter of St Benedict's rule (*c*.1100). The Cistercians were a particularly important order in Wales.

Bohun, Humphrey de   The seventh of that name, *c*.1250–98, *Marcher lord* of Brecknock.

Bondmen   The lower orders in Welsh society consisting of those whose position was roughly equivalent to that of the *villein*. Their freedom was restricted and they provided labour services.

Bruce, Robert   The sixth (1210–95). Claimant to the Scottish throne, assented to the marriage of Princess Margaret of Scotland to Edward, Prince of Wales, and the Union of England with Scotland, 1290.

Brutus   The legendary founder of the Britons in Britain.

Burgage   Property within a borough held by a burgess by payment of rent to the lord.

Burgess   A person with rights and property within a borough.

Cantred/cantref   An administrative division in medieval Wales based on a notional 'hundred townships'.

Carucate   A unit of land, usually 120 acres.

Ceisiad   A community police officer, the sergeant of the peace, as opposed to the *rhingyll*, who was an officer of the court.

Chancery   An issuing house and repository for government legal documents.

Chapter   The canons of a cathedral acting as a management committee.

Cilmeri   Site of the death of Llywelyn the Last, Prince of Wales, on 11 December 1282.

Clare, Gilbert de   The fourth of that name in the de Clare dynasty, 1243–95. Known as 'the Red Earl'. Sided in turn with the two

Llywelyns and with the English king. *Marcher lord* of Glamorgan and one of the most powerful men in Wales.

Commote/cwmwd A division of a *cantref*: the optimum administrative unit in medieval Wales.

Concentric Castles went through various stages of development from simple 'motte and bailey' constructions to the vast stone edifices constructed in Wales during the thirteenth century which are considered in this book. The concentric plan in the great Welsh castles involved the principle of successive lines of defence so that each 'ward' or section of the castle was placed wholly within another. The outermost defence was the *curtain wall*, surrounding the whole castle, studded with protective towers. The entrance to the castle was protected by moat, ditch, drawbridge and portcullis. The portcullis was operated within a massive *gatehouse*, which was flanked by great stone towers and could house troops.

Croes Naid The most cherished relic of independent Wales, the piece of the True Cross removed by Edward I after conquest.

Curia The administrative and clerical staff of a medieval state, so called because they were clergy, like the administrative staff of the papacy.

Curtain walling The outermost defence of the castle. See *Concentric*.

Curtilage The land adjoining a burgage tenement.

Dafydd ap Gruffudd Prince of Gwynedd. Third son of Gruffudd ap Llywelyn, younger brother of Llywelyn ap Gruffudd. Bitterly hostile to his brother Llywelyn (the Last); fought against the English after the death of Llywelyn in 1282. Executed by King Edward I in 1283.

Demesne Land legally possessed by an owner except for that held by freehold tenants.

Distain A steward or *seneschal* in Welsh administration; in

	Gwynedd he was the effective first minister of the prince.
Dominicans	One of the great mendicant orders of friars. Founded by St Dominic (1221). (See also *Franciscans*.)
Dower	A widow's share of her late husband's property.
Entrepôt	A centre, usually a port, for the collection, storage, shipment and distribution of goods.
Exchequer	The Crown's principal financial department, a term applied to similar functions in the lordships.
Excommunication	Exclusion from the sacrament of the Church.
Extents	Surveys of land, in this instance for the purpose of exacting rents.
Eyre	Circuit court held by justices.
Fealty	An oath sworn to one's lord promising faithful service as part of an act of homage.
Feudalism	A social structure and system of land tenure based on the equation of landholding with military responsibility. The king granted land to his *tenants-in-chief* in return for military service and they infeudated their knights and retainers, while the actual farm work would be done by unfree labourers in return for the use of some land for themselves.
Food render	A tax of foodstuffs upon a community for the maintenance of the court or one of its officers.
Franchise	A full, legally recognized right, for example that pertaining to burgesses within a medieval borough.
Franciscans	One of the great mendicant orders of friars. Founded by St Francis (1226) who provided inspiration for other mendicant orders in his stress on members having the absolute minimum of personal possessions so the friars could preach to the poorest and humblest.
Freeholder	A person who owned land free of feudal services or rent.

Gatehouses	See under *Concentric*.
Giraldus Cambrensis/ Gerald of Wales	*c.*1146–1223. Archdeacon of Brecon. Undertook famous itinerary around Wales in 1188 with Bishop Baldwin to recruit soldiers for the third crusade. Resulted in one of the most important of medieval source writings, the *Itinerarium Kambriae* (*The Journey through Wales*). Great proponent of independence of see of St Davids from Canterbury.
Homage	A formal act to show that one is submitting to the feudal authority of an overlord.
Indemnity	A sum paid as compensation for loss or by one party in a conflict to another to secure peace.
Indulgences	In Roman Catholicism, remission of purgatorial atonement for sin secured by canonical penance.
Ingeniator	Literally, engineer.
Interdict	A church decree depriving groups of people or communities of all church services and sacraments. The Pope imposed a full interdict on King John's England from 1208–14.
Kindred	An extended family group, legally recognized in Welsh law up to seven degrees of relationships.
Knight's fee	A parcel of land for the tenure of which the holder provided one armed knight for the lord's military service.
Knights Hospitallers	Knights Hospitallers and *Knights Templars* were religious orders created at the beginning of the twelfth century. They were military orders arising out of the religious wars of Christendom against Islam in the Holy Land and in Spain.
Knights Templars	See *Knights Hospitallers*.
Laws of Hywel Dda	Hywel Dda, died 950, ruler of Ceredigion and Ystrad Tywi. Initiated the codification of Welsh laws in the tenth century, although the first extant manuscript of

the laws is from the twelfth century. Welsh law was vital to a sense of Welsh nationality before the conquest.

Llywelyn ab Iorwerth — Llywelyn the Great, Prince of Gwynedd, 1173–1240, often styled Llywelyn I.

Llywelyn Bren — Died 1317. Led a major revolt in Glamorgan against Edward II but it lasted only a few weeks.

Maerdref — The estate around a hamlet.

Marcher lords — Originally Norman lords who had settled on the border between England and Wales and who acquired land by westward advance and conquest.

Maredudd ap Rhys Gryg — Died 1272. Prince of Deheubarth.

Metes and bounds — Boundaries.

Mesne tenant — An intermediate tenant, whose grant of land from his overlord had been let to a sub-tenant, but who still owed feudal service for that land to the overlord (*mesne lord*).

Montfort, Simon de — c.1208–65. Became Earl of Leicester. Married Eleanor, sister of Henry III in 1238. Leader of barons' revolt against the King, whom he defeated in 1264 at the Battle of Lewes. Defeated by royal forces, including *Marcher lords*, at the Battle of Evesham 1265. Llywelyn ap Gruffudd married Simon de Montfort's daughter, Eleanor, in 1278.

Mortimer, Roger — Died 1282. One of the great adversaries of Llywelyn ap Gruffudd who defeated Mortimer in 1262 and 1266, obtaining substantial areas of Mortimer lands by the Treaty of Montgomery 1267.

Oratory — A small private chapel.

Pannage — The right of pasturing pigs in a forest or payment made for this.

Papal indult — Licence or permission granted by the Pope authorizing something to be done which the law of the Church did not sanction.

Partible inheritance	The equal division of hereditary property among the heirs.
Plantaganet	Surname given to the Angevin line of kings descended from Geoffrey, Count of Anjou. The Plantaganets ruled England from 1154 to 1485. Henry II was the first Plantaganet king.
Prid	A convoluted way of buying land in spite of the Welsh law's strictures against permanent alienation of land. The land was placed with the 'buyer' as notional security for a sum of money which was given to the 'vendor' on the tacit understanding that the money would not be repaid and the land never reclaimed.
Proctors	Officials representing others in a legal capacity.
Quinzaine	Fifteen days after or before.
Quitclaim	A disclaimer of all legal rights and interests.
Reliefs	Sums paid by an heir to his lord in order to secure succession to his predecessor's land.
Rhaglaw	The deputy of the king or lord in Welsh law.
Rhingyll	The sergeant-at-law in a Welsh court who acted as a security officer during court sittings.
Rhys ap Maredudd	1132–97. Yr Arglwydd Rhys — or the Lord Rhys. The leading Welsh magnate of the period.
Saracens	Name given to the Muhammadans of Syria and Palestine. Later used to denote all infidel nations against whom crusades were preached.
Scriptorium	The manuscript copying and illuminating section of a monastic house: the copying was often done in open carrels in the cloister rather than in a special room.
Seigneurial	Pertaining to a feudal lord rather than to the king.
Seised	In legal possession of property.

Seneschal	Official in household of prince to whom control of justice and administration was given.
Sheriff	The principal royal official in English shires, introduced into Wales after the conquest.
Siege train	The equipment required by an army to cut off all outside communication and supplies to a castle or town, so compelling surrender.
Subsidy	A form of taxation for a specified purpose.
Supplication	Appeals to God through prayer, usually for the forgiveness of sins and the release of souls from purgatory.
Tenant-in-chief	A magnate holding land directly from the king, as Llywelyn and the greater earls did.
Union legislation	The Acts of 1536 and 1543 whereby England and Wales were united under the law, administration and language prevailing in England.
Vassal	A person who acknowledged another as an overlord and was bound by obligations to that overlord.
Villein	An unfree agricultural peasant, bound to provide labour service for his lord in return for a small land holding.
Vivaries	Game enclosures.
Welshry	A community, within a royal shire, governed according to Welsh law.

Index